DISCARDED FROM THE COLLECTION

CITY OF OAKLAND

OAKLAND PUBLIC LIBRARY
OAKLAND, CA

MOSAICS
An Anthology of Creative Writings by Seniors

Edited by
Jennifer D. King
and
Jean Mundy

DIMOND BRANCH LIBRARY
3565 FRUITVALE AVENUE
OAKLAND, CALIF. 94602

A project of the Creative Writing Classes
of the Downtown Oakland Senior Center
and West Oakland Senior Center
With Contributions from
the Senior Writing Community
across the Country
2010

Copyright © 2010
Downtown Oakland and West Oakland
Senior Center Writing Classes

All rights reserved. This book, or parts thereof,
may not be reproduced in any form without permission.

Funding for MOSAICS

"Generosity consists not the sum given,
but the manner in which it is bestowed"
Mahatma Gandhi

The creative writing workshop members, staff, and Advisory Councils of the Downtown and West Oakland Senior Centers gratefully acknowledge the generous funding provided by all of our donors. Their donations provided the "wind beneath the wings" of the writers, and made this project possible. We sincerely appreciate your continued support.

Oakland Rotary
Oakland Black Firefighters Association
DOSC Advisory Council
Delta Sigma Theta Sorority
DOSC Book Club

DOWNTOWN OAKLAND SENIOR CENTER WRITING CLASSES

"Will the reader get it?" It's a question that arises again and again in any creative writing class or workshop. The writers create a piece, but that's the easy part. Then come the endless revisions and attempts to ensure that the intent is clear and the writing polished. The writing process is time consuming and often frustrating. The writer, however, has no choice. Writing that moves, provokes, enthralls, and captivates the reader doesn't just happen - it is the result of a process. While creativity is innate, craftsmanship is a result of hard work.

Participation in creative writing classes and workshops offer senior writers an opportunity to hone their craft along with fellow writers. The Downtown Oakland Senior Center currently offers three creative writing classes,

Fiction/Memoir – This group meets monthly. The class is free and is open to all serious writers of fiction and memoirs. The class is led by Mark Greenside. Mark is the author of a collection of short stories, *I Saw a Man Hit His Wife*, and a memoir/travelogue, *I'll Never Be French*.

Poetry – This free workshop meets the 1st, 2nd, and 4th Friday mornings at 9:30. Jennifer King is the facilitator.

Creative Non-Fiction – This class meets every Friday morning at 8:30 and is open to writers of all levels.

WEST OAKLAND SENIOR CENTER CREATIVE WRITING WORKSHOP

Write On!, a creative writing workshop for seniors has been in existence for over five years. The workshop is designed for those seniors wishing to explore their creativity through the written word. Class members work on a variety of genres: poetry, essays, and short stories. The collective wisdom of the group continues to be their greatest asset.

In 2008, the workshop, then eleven members, published Potter's Clay. In this brilliant collection of short stories about their parents, workshop members shared the memories of their mothers and fathers told against the backdrop of World Wars, the Great Depression, Harlem Renaissance, and the turbulent Sixties. In Potter's Clay, hilarity and tragedy, laughter and tears were skillfully woven through the fabric of celebratory tales that allow the reader to view their parents as the loving and caring, though deeply flawed people they actually were.

The Write On! workshop sessions foster creativity and self-expression in a supportive learning environment. The workshop meets at 10:00 every Friday morning. The writing workshop sessions are free and open to all senior writers and would-be writers.

MOSAICS EDITORS

JENNIFER D. KING

The proud director of the Downtown Oakland Senior Center was born in Florida and raised in New Jersey. Jennifer attended Mills College where she earned her Bachelors and Masters degrees in English. She is also an Adjunct Professor of English for the Peralta Community College District, and at the Allen Temple Leadership Institute. Jennifer teaches the Friday Morning Poetry Class at the Downtown Oakland Senior Center. She is passionate about writing! Her poetry, short stories and essays have appeared in a number of local and national publications. *Turning My Face to the Sun*, a compilation of her poems and short stories, was published in 2007. Additionally, she has written Christian Education materials for Urban Ministries, Inc. for twelve years. Jennifer is an avid reader and loves travelling.

JEAN MUNDY

Jean Mundy was born and reared on a farm on the Eastern Shore of Maryland. After attending business school in Delaware she worked for an advertising agency as a secretary and proof reader for ten years, then married and moved to California. For seventeen years she worked for a trade advertising agency in Oakland, and finally ended her working career after fifteen years with the City of Oakland as an Administrative Assistant.

Jean's takes tap dancing and singing classes, enjoys reading, keeping up with current events, and socializing. She is a long-time office volunteer at the Downtown Oakland Senior Center.

FOREWORD

There is a lovely generosity in memory. While we read the stories, poems, memoirs and vignettes of each of these writers in *Mosaics*, very personal memories emerge: of visits to far away places, a father singing Chinese opera, the birthing of a child or the prospect of dying alone. Each is lyrical, filtered through the lens of wisdom, time, love and some humor.

Although the details of each of these works are personal to the lives of the writers, in them, we find our own lives. We share with the writers the perspective of their experiences and recognize the journeys they take as stirring up new understandings of our own voyages. What does a young child feel when her father breaks into song in their restaurant? Don't we all recognize that embarrassment of our own oddness? Or how you make a promise that is almost impossible to keep? Or find it important to break with a friend?

The chapters of our lives have twists and turns that sometimes render a sense of loneliness. In writing we gift our memories to others allowing a collective remembering and a joining of the emotions that both move and paralyze us. The writers in *Mosaics* forge the individual pieces of their lives to create a picture all of us can see. Despite their different colors, sizes and qualities, we step back and remember. All of it is there: in the tradition of Sunday church, the appreciation of old men, of the irony of life, like the tchotchkes on the shelf, cataloguing the treasures of the relationships to the heart and mind.

The originality and life of these writings bring a sparkle to the stones of the *Mosaics*. The stories and poems afford a resonance that we can relate to. We are reminded as one writer said, Death and life, death and life, round and round.

Congratulations to the writers and to the program directors. Treasure each particle, each stone and the pictures they create.

Elmaz Abinader

MOSAICS
Andrea Youngdahl

As I sat reading the luminous stories and poems that will make up this fourth anthology of writings by those of us over 50, I applauded whoever chose the title *"Mosaics"*. Mosaic – is an ancient art form from B.C. and beyond, involving bits and pieces of glass, stone, ceramic and now digital images making up a beautiful whole. Mosaics - like a life lived – small pieces, memories, moments, images that collectively make up larger images and define the work of art we call our life, our story, our poem.

Contained in these precious pages are literary mosaics from more than 50 writers representing six different states. The journeys they take us on range from painful pictures of loss, domestic abuse, and the difficulties of immigration to the joyful yet complicated images of birth, love, family and friendship. Perhaps it's my roots in the rebellious sixties and seventies that made me laugh and celebrate the poem about the *"80 year old James Dean"*. And it is my love of beautifully written lines that stay with me long after finishing a story made me read this phrase at least five times: "My friend and I were gurgling streams of consciousness, with rocks to grab with our toes so that we did what needed doing in daily life."

The beauty of writing from the perspective of age fills every page of this anthology. Existential angst is replaced by murmurings and exaltations of life's moments – precious treasures that combine into an intricate pattern. One turns the pages, encountering difficult journeys, celebrations of survival, cups of coffee and childhood images evolved into touchstones for aging. As one story quotes from the dramatist Lorraine Hansbury: "the WHY of why we're here is an intrigue for adolescents; the HOW is what must command the living."

Finally, we are reminded that every day brings blessings. And while the years may have ended our innocence and cleared our illusions, we are nurtured by that which we touch and that which we can only imagine:

"Today the earth is sweet, the sun warm. I've planted tomatoes. I haven't planted tomatoes in 35 years. The deer may win out or the squirrels but today there is hope that the warm sun will illuminate the genetic system of those leafy stems. The aroma of those sturdy rich green stems and leaves fill my nostrils, and the small confines of the weed tufted patch of yard are a momentary altar to well being. The planet spins as the Hubble telescope up there, so far away up there above us, sucks in the beauty of the bigger universe which is really just another pinprick in a larger fabric. Glorious high tech Hubble space photos will soon grace a million gift shop windows. I hanker after them."

And I know you will hanker after the work within. With deepest gratitude to the authors who have chosen to share their mosaics with all of us.

Andrea Youngdahl, Director
Department of Human Services
City of Oakland

TABLE OF CONTENTS

BETH AALAND
Mosaic of Shapes and Colors 2
Can a Doodler be Called an Artist? 4

ANN-MARIE ASKEW
Coming Home 6
My Gleaner 9
Geovani the Gigolo 12
Reunion 15

BILLIE THOMPSON BAILEY
It Shouldn't Have Happened But It Did 17

SREELA BANERJEE
Every Cloud Has A Silver Lining 18

GILBERT BENDIX
(Not So) Far Away Places 19
Knowledge 20

RUTH BENNETT
The General Wishes Another Handwriting Sample 21

GIOVANNA CAPONE
To America 28
Rush Hour In Manhattan For My Sister Rose 30
A Place at the Table 32

GERE CHERRY
My Reflection In The Pond 37

PEARL CHINN
Fear of Living 39
Places to Sleep 40

RAYMOND CHOW
The Interplay of Words: 42
I Found My Inner Peace 44
Restoration of Faith With Mankind 45

DOUGLAS E. COLEMAN
The Yearning Heart 46
The Troubling Oceans 47

KEN COLEMAN
Untitled 52

CYNTHIA DRORI
Finger Prints at a Nazi Primary 53

TABLE OF CONTENTS

MARILYN DUMESNIL
   The Salubrious Sea 55
LUCY ELY
   Why I Stopped Smoking 56
CAROL L. EVANS
   Mama Won't You Play For Me Just One More Time 57
   Returning Home On The California Zephyr 58
   The Traveling Heart 63
LUCY RAU FERGUSON
   Villaremi: A Family Memoir..66
   Kate's Wine 69
MAIMIE GIMBLE
   Aunt Katy's New Hobby 75
JOYCE GUBELMAN
   The Brown Chair...77
   Some Fish! 78
   Sanong and Me..80
RUTH GUTHARTZ
   Tchotchkes 83
BETSY HESS-BEHRENS
   Chicken Checkmate 87
   The Diamond Ring..91
ROY M. KAHN
   Capri: A Slide Show – Italy, 1935 95
   On Doing the Laundry 96
   Rented 97
   Stalag X - 1945 99
   Untitled..100
JENNIFER D. KING
   In Praise of Older Men 101
   A Cure...102
   We are Like Children 103
   Sorry, I don't Understand 104
   Domestic Disturbance 105
JULAINA KLEIST
   His Seeds 110

TABLE OF CONTENTS

RITA LABRIE
  Memories of France 112
  Dementia 113
ELEANOR LEVINE
  Birthing Nate (An Essay) 114
NADA LIGHT
  A Bird in a Cage 117
JOY LUCADELLO LUSTER
  A Time of Hope 121
  Getting Ready 126
  Woman 131
JESSIE MCELROY-THRASH
  Stories and Tales 132
  Sunday Church Train 133
  Imagination 134
  It's Almost Here 135
SALLY A. MILLER
  Mosaic Home 136
GAYLE MOHRBACKER
  Part One: Living in the Present 138
KHALEEDAH MUHAMMAD
  Grandma Winnie's Hand's 142
  Thoughts! 147
  Sand Pebbles 148
  Sertia's Journey 149
WANDA NG
  In Hot Pursuit 154
HILDY PEHRSON
  My Life's Bouquet 159
  Manzanar 160
REME F. PICK
  I Am a Tropical Beauty 161
PAT PURVIS
  My Arms Ache 163
  My Family's Mosaic 166
ELODIA B. RESENDEZ
  Texas Good Man 169

TABLE OF CONTENTS

BELINDA RICKLEFS
On the Road to Vera Cruz 171
PAT ROPER
Age Strong! Live Long! 177
IRENE SARDANIS
Sacred Space 179
Singing 180
CLAUDE SHAVER
What If? 183
Autumn Glory 184
TONIA L. STANLEY
At The Table 185
JOANNE SULTAR
In Miami When I Took A Walk 188
Map of Miami 189
The Payroll 190
Uncle Meyer's Request 191
MEI SUN LI
The Czarina Sleeps In 193
Once Upon A Time 194
MARY TATE
No Harm Done – Part 1 197
No Harm Done – Part 2 202
Out to the Sylvesters - A Trip to Nostalgia 208
ARDITH THOMPSON
Rhode Island Reds and Me 209
Taking A Risk 210
BOLA THOMPSON
Love 212
TERRANCE TOUCHETT
Legacy of a Wanderer: The Guitar Playing Man 213
The Sound of Humanity 218
Have a Great Day 220
A Shopping I'll Go 221
Circus 222

TABLE OF CONTENTS

ANKE VAN AARDENNE
Sleepless Nights 223
Rural Holland 224
Room With A Skeleton 225

BARBARA AKOSUA WILLIAMS
Must Say Good-bye 229
Visits 231
Sometimes 232

BARBARA J. WILLIAMS
Explorations in Equity 233
Joy 236
New Years Eve at the Senior Care Unit 237
Mother's Lambs 239

VALENA M. WILLIAMS (SR.)
August In Paris 240

KRISTINA YATES
I Know You 246
'Normal' 247

ANDREA YEE
Diner 251

MOSAICS
An Anthology of Creative Writings by Seniors

MOSAIC OF SHAPES AND COLOR
Beth Aaland

Life is a kaleidoscope.
Shapes touching
and pulling apart.
Colors gleaming, fading,
gleaming again.

Associations always there,
seen and unseen
only to sink away. Then to come again
eons from now.

There is no combination of shapes and colors
that remain forever apart.
There is no end.

In Norway nineteen sixty-six
Ninety-year-old Tante Karen and I touch hands
the colors of my life soften
and sharp edges become smooth.
Our lives mesh together for the minutes
we come to know each other.

My cousin and I swim together in Lake Tvara.
We speak as we swim.
Yellow and orange are our words
pyramid shapes of green trees on the shore
surround us and soothe our souls.
In her time my cousin leaves this earth.

More combinations
surround my life.
Colors and shapes spiral on.

Norway, summer two thousand eight
Combinations are changing
my son and family are here.

I visit them.
The faded colors of my life brighten.
Shapes become sharper
as I remember how much love
there is in this world.
I feel young again.

We drive up the hill where the antelopes stay
on either side of the road.
The building is no longer a home for
old folks,
it has become apartment dwellings
for refugees.

I meet and hug Geel and her husband, Ahmad.
We speak together and
share a little of our lives.
Iran is their home.
Sadly, now they don't know where they are going
they don't know who will welcome them.

The colors in my life fade a little.
I cry.
My shape wilts and droops.

We drive to Lake Tvara. We cannot swim.
A swamp overwhelms the bridge
that leads to the lake.
We hold hands and weep a little.
I remember my cousin and our words
of yellow and orange.
Now Geel, Ahmad and I speak misty-grey
worry words.

Again I remind myself
of my belief:
Life is a kaleidoscope,
change is forever.

CAN A DOODLER BE CALLED AN ARTIST?
Beth Aaland

The dictionary definition of doodle is "to scribble absentmindedly, engage in idle activity, or a rough drawing made absentmindedly." The origin of the noun, from the early 17th century, denoted a fool, or the verb was used "to make a fool of," or to "cheat." In present time there is a question about whether the result of doodling is an art form. Can one say that art can be a result of sub-consciousness when someone is daydreaming, bored or loses interest in his conscious activity? There is some controversy about the definition of art. If mosaics, a three-dimensional puzzle, in different materials, is considered an art form, then doodling as a form of two- dimensional expression may also be considered art. Naturally, when one defines art as all conscious, creative activity, one may conclude that doodling is a form of art. So, can one say that a doodler is in fact an artist just as one who develops mosaics?

I doodle unconsciously when I am on the telephone waiting for a human being to answer. I do it whenever there happens to be paper, pencil, and flat surface around. My doodles are lines, curvy, straight, spirals without thought. I do not start with a conscious idea of what I am going to paint or draw. I believe the left side of my brain is working as I make squiggles or join lines together unconsciously.

I have watched students who have doodled their unconscious creations while listening to lectures. If I were Carl Jung, the psychiatrist, maybe I could translate the message and interpret the child's personality. Perhaps, the truth is that the only one who can really interpret the doodle coming from the left side of the brain is the person doing the doodling. Doodles can often result in problem solving, presumably after the left side of the brain has become active during the doodling process.

My friend, who has a reputation for being a true artist, uses paint, brushes, and canvas. She experiences different kinds of emotion as she paints. She enjoys paint smells, the feel of the canvas, the ideas and pictures that she wants to recreate and share with an audience. She also has a notion about what she intends to paint, and is able to judge whether her creation has met her right brain specifications.

She thinks in a logical, straightforward way and has little or no desire to doodle. However, she does concede that some doodles might be considered art.

Doodles can also be created on the computer with a program called Photoshop Elements. This aspect of drawing is another step away from the absentminded line creations used with pencil and paper.

My absentminded scribble can also be applied when I use a mouse to draw any lines my hand-eye coordination chooses.

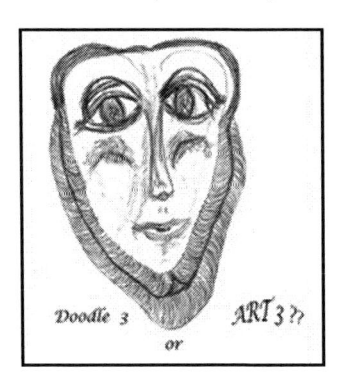

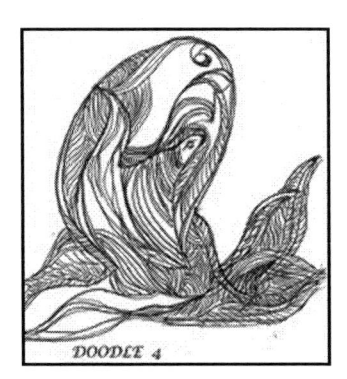

Doodle 3 or ART 3 ??

DOODLE 4

However, there is a machine in the path between brain and fingers. I am not so happy with my machine doodle. I don't feel quite so involved. I understand the attitude of my friend who feels uncomfortable painting or drawing without the accouterments she has become used to.

After I have looked at my doodle creation I transfer the art symbols I have doodled into right brain ideas, which I call creative logic or poetry. I have grown several poems which I believe came into my consciousness from the unconscious design of the symbols I put together in my doodle.

I have finally come to believe doodling can be considered an art form, similar to folk art.

"Every artist dips his brush in his own soul
and paints his own nature into his pictures."

Henry Ward Beecher

COMING HOME
Ann-Marie Askew

Fifty years after leaving Oakland at age twenty, I longed to return to my roots. In Eugene, Oregon, I didn't have the financial or physical means to maintain my house and overgrown yard. I couldn't afford to replace the moss-laden roof and unstable foundation, nor climb an extension ladder to trim the laurel hedge that threatened to encapsulate my little homestead. I dreaded splitting firewood for my primary source of heat and feared the water pipes would freeze as in previous years. But mainly I missed living among people who had various skin hues or spoke languages other than English. I wanted to be a tile in Oakland's multi-ethnic mosaic.

I'd lived with my sixteen-year-old cat longer than any of my three husbands, but she stopped eating in July 2009 and died soon thereafter. Completely alone for the first time ever, I thought about how my daughter's kids in Eugene were now more into their friends than Grandma, but how my son's three-year-old was soon to get a baby brother in San Francisco, where access to Grandma would be greatly appreciated. So even though the economy was in recession, I put my Eugene house on the market.

Miraculously, I got an offer within a few weeks. Thinking I had a sure sale, I drove to Oakland and put a deposit on a Lake Merritt apartment. However, on October 20th, the buyer withdrew and retrieved his earnest money. Uh, oh. What now?

Potential buyers generally loved the neighborhood but were discouraged by the "as-is" condition of my house. On November 20th I received TWO offers--one much too low. I countered the other, and we agreed that the buyer would pay for an extensive inspection if I'd commit $2500 toward repair costs. He was a fifty-year-old opera singer with a deep, resonant voice. I liked him.

He wanted the sale to close before the end of the year, but since I planned to drive to San Francisco in mid-December to be granny-in-residence for several weeks after my daughter-in-law gave birth, he agreed that I wouldn't have to move out until January 15th. Everything was falling into place!

But then the temperature dropped to nine degrees, freezing the pipes and drains in the bath and laundry rooms, and my daughter-in-law went into labor a week early. So I drove cautiously off my icy hillside onto I-5, pleased to leave my inhospitable house for San Francisco's milder climate, but concerned the pipes might burst and kill the sale in my absence.

When the Eugene temperature finally rose above freezing a few days later, my daughter reported that the pipes were intact, but she and her husband replaced a leaking bathroom sink hose. I tried not to worry about my house as I played with and read to my granddaughter, shopped and prepared meals, did laundry, and cooed over my gorgeous new grandson.

The contractor found additional dry rot on the roof, increasing the repair cost to $2770, which I agreed to pay. The appraisal came in at value, and when the escrow officer e-mailed to me the closing documents, I signed and returned them the day after Christmas. Then I went house hunting in Oakland again and fell in love with a fifth floor Art Deco apartment. Within walking distance of my father's 15th Street tailor shop—now, half a century later, a hip-hop shop—its fourteen tall windows overlook the hills where I grew up. After telling the apartment manager that I'd let him know as soon as my house sale closed, I stopped at a nearby Internet cafe where several dozen African-Americans of all ages were celebrating the first day of Kwansa. Their friendly smiles made me feel welcome, and I hoped with all my heart that I'd be able to share their community soon.

However, my opera singing buyer did NOT sign the closing documents. He decided that the contractor's spot treatment for wood-boring beetles wasn't sufficient and demanded to have the entire house treated at my expense, even though I had already agreed to pay several hundred dollars over our original contract.

Exhausted from trying to please the prima donna, and unwilling to invest more money in the house I intended to sell, I decided to sing the closing aria to the now tragic opera myself. So I responded that unless he signs the closing documents immediately, the sale is dead.

However, the curtain didn't come down after I retreated into the audience. The prima donna remounted the stage for a grande finale and authorized the escrow officer to close the sale. I stood up, applauded, and cheered!

It was December 30, an auspicious day. The day my father was born in 1900, the day my parents married in 1928, and in 2009, two weeks after my seventieth birthday, the day I knew I'd return to Oakland after an absence of fifty years.

That afternoon I gave the Art Deco apartment manager a deposit, then met my daughter and her kids where they'd been visiting over the holidays. We walked to the Chapel of the Chimes to visit the remains of my parents, shelved in a magical crevice. As my grandkids played hide-and-seek among the ferns, lilies, and cherubic statuary, I thanked my mom and dad for giving me life.

After I returned to Eugene to pack up and move out, the buyer came over to show the house to relatives, and we didn't mention our recent financial haggling. Although I thought I'd witnessed the final act of our opera, a month later he sent me an e-mail requesting that I remove scrap lumber from under the back deck and a file cabinet in the storage shed. WHAT? Doesn't he get it that the curtain came down and the audience went HOME? I ignored his e-mail and didn't hear from him again. This is the time for my OWN final act, here in Oakland, where my opera started over seventy years ago.

MY GLEANER
Ann-Marie Askew

With a helicopter again encircling my downtown Oakland neighborhood, I feared a repeat of last week's street violence that followed in the wake of the involuntary manslaughter verdict for the shooting of a prone, unarmed black man by a white cop. The helicopter seemed to be focused on a section of freeway about a mile from my apartment, so I walked over to find out what was happening. A bystander told me that a lone white man from out of town, clad in a bullet-resistant vest, had opened gunfire on two highway patrolmen in the middle of the night. The shooter had at least three guns and lots of ammunition in his pick-up truck. More than twelve hours later the freeway was still closed as bomb squad technicians and the FBI searched his truck and gathered evidence. My curiosity satisfied, I headed home.

As I approached my apartment building, a man across the street called out, "Hello, mon, nice day!" I turned to see one of the few people in my neighborhood who make eye contact, much less say anything to me, so I waved and returned his warm greeting. Standing next to a grocery cart overflowing with large, lumpy, black plastic bags, he's the guy I sometimes see sorting through garbage containers below my fifth floor apartment window. He never leaves a mess, carefully replacing what he doesn't take. Most remarkably, he's usually clad in one of his ubiquitous black plastic bags.

On impulse I crossed the street and said, "I'd like to ask you a question," as he stepped towards me, cigarette in hand. He was wearing a decent looking shirt and pants, not a black plastic bag.

"Sure, mon, it really is a nice day!" he said with a broad grin that revealed several missing teeth in his dark, middle-aged face. His classic features and winning smile actually reminded me of my youngest son's father who'd also spent time on the streets. But this guy didn't seem to be drunk or high on drugs.

"I'm just wondering what it is you're looking for in the trash," I said. "Our apartment manager has us leave recyclables inside, so the pickings from my building across the street aren't very useful, I'm afraid."

"Oh, but I always find a few bottles and cans anyhow."

"Well, if you're going to be here a few more minutes, I can bring out my recyclables. I have some beer bottles and a few other things."

"I'll be here. I'm just on a cigarette break," he said, still grinning. "And you know what I could really use is a peanut-butter and jam sandwich, if you could do that for me."

"Humm. Actually I don't know if I have peanut-butter or jam. But I'll bring you something."

"Syrup would be good on peanut-butter," he said. "That is, if you don't have jam."

"Okay, don't go away. I'll be right back," I said, starting back across the street.

"Oh, I'll be here, mon. I'll be here."

As I rode the elevator, I decided to bring him some of the black bean chili I'd made last night. So I spooned several helpings into a yogurt container with leftover brown rice. While it heated in the microwave, I added the six-pack of empty beer bottles to the tin cans, plastic containers, and wine bottles I'd accumulated in a Whole Foods paper sack. Then I placed the container of warmed chili in a plastic bag with a plastic fork.

My dinner guest met me in front of my building. Handing him the two bags, I explained that I didn't have any peanut-butter, but brought him some chili that I'd made last night. "It's really good," I said.

"Did you heat it up?" he asked, reaching into the plastic bag to touch its plastic container.

"Of course. I hope you enjoy it."

"Did you put sugar on it? I always like it to be sweet."

"Well, no," I said, wondering where this was going.

"Would you mind doing that? And maybe a slice of bread. Or some crackers." He handed me back the plastic bag with the chili inside.

"Okay," I said. "I'll be right back."

So I went back up my elevator, poured some sugar into a sandwich baggie, not wanting to defile my delicious chili, and found an unopened bag of rice crackers.

"Oh, thank you, mon," he said, patting my arm as I handed him the food.

"Have you always lived in Oakland?" I asked. "Or are you from someplace else?" I didn't detect a Jamaican accent, but noted that he addressed me as "mon."

"Oh yeah," he said, putting a hand on my arm again. His gentle touch was as inoffensive as his warm, gap-toothed smile. "Been here since I was a little boy. Came from Fresno originally."

"Do you have a place to live?" I asked, fearing what I might hear.

"Of course. In West Oakland. My mother keeps wanting me to move in with her out near 77th. But I don't want to go back to living with my mother, if you know what I mean."

"I understand," I said. "Well, it's been nice talking to you. And I appreciate your friendliness. Keep smiling."

"Thank you, mon. It's a beautiful day!"

About half an hour later I heard him rattling around in the garbage containers below my window. I peeked out to see him clad in a black plastic bag. And the helicopter was still encircling the neighborhood.

GEOVANI THE GIGOLO
Ann-Marie Askew

At age sixty-one I took an Elderhostel trip to Costa Rica that included walking, hiking, cycling, swimming, river rafting, and kayaking. The brochure didn't mention having sex. I was one of sixteen participants at least fifty-five years old: four heterosexual couples, six single women, each traveling with a sister or close friend, one single man--and me.

As our group prepared to river raft in a heavily misted rain forest, our river guide insisted on helping me put on my life jacket. *"Un momento por favor,"* the cute guy less than half my age said, running his fingers through my shoulder-length gray hair. When he intimately popped a blackhead between my shoulder blades, I realized that Geovani was FLIRTING with me! That evening he told me to let him know next time I come to Costa Rico – alone, so he can pick me up at the airport in his Land Rover to give me a SPECIAL tour. I just laughed, assuming he'd get the message that I'm not interested in sharing my body–or my money–with him, although it felt good to be noticed as a sexual being, instead of being an invisible "older woman".

Then at the dinner table a few nights later one of the other single women said that Geovani had massaged her shoulders on the deck outside her cabin and told her she's juicy, his hard-on knocking against her butt. When she told him she's with her girlfriend, he responded that he can do whatever she can do only better. So I shared my story, and we laughed about Geovani "two-timing" us. Betty and I agreed that on some level we were flattered, the young guy's attention making us feel sexually attractive in spite of the decades we had on him.

However, I'd been thinking about how his behavior was potentially dangerous to women less experienced than Betty or me. Naïve, lonely women might interpret his attention as genuine affection, then give him money. After all, Elderhostel participants don't sign up for a sex tour. So at the end of our trip I reported his behavior on a written evaluation form, indicating that I'd be willing to discuss the situation if someone at Elderhostel or the rafting company wanted to follow-up.

About two months after the trip, my phone rang early one morning. To my immense surprise, it was Geovani calling from Costa Rica. In broken English, he angrily said that he hasn't been able to work since I reported him to Elderhostel, and he wants me to do something about it. Uh, oh, I thought. I didn't think he'd get fired! I just thought they'd give him a warning!

I asked how he got my phone number. He said from my son. From my son? Before I could question him further, he ranted about how he hadn't done anything wrong, and he needs to work to support his family.

Trembling, I tried to keep my voice even as I told him I reported him because his behavior was inappropriate: he'd made sexual overtures to me and Betty, who are at least thirty years older than him, and I believe he did so because he thinks we have money to spend on him. I said that women don't go on Elderhostel trips to be approached by a gigolo, and I don't want other women to be put in that situation.

I don't think he understood what I said because he responded that his English is not very good, and he plans to take some classes.

"Your English isn't the problem," I said. "You made it very clear to me and to Betty what you wanted."

Then he asked where I'd been sitting on the raft. Apparently he didn't remember me! Obviously Betty and I weren't the only women he hit on. He probably focuses on one or more single women from every tourist group he floats down the river—and can't tell us apart!

"Geovani," I said. "I'm going to hang up because I have to go to work."

He begged me to send a letter to the rafting company stating that he should get his job back. Instead, I sent an e-mail to our Elderhostel tour guide, describing Geovani's phone call and asking how he got my son's phone number.

I never did hear from the tour guide, so I phoned Elderhostel and talked to a man who handles program evaluations. He said he was shocked that Geovani had my personal information and promised he'd investigate and get back to me, claiming that in his fourteen years on the job, nothing like this had ever happened. I doubted that, but perhaps other women don't report gigolo encounters. A week later he called back to say he thinks Geovani got my son's phone number from the next-of-kin form I signed for the rafting company.

Although I felt badly that Geovani was out of work, I thought he shouldn't have access to older women with potential money to spend on him. Especially not older women who don't want to feel sexually interchangeable.

REUNION
Ann-Marie Askew

Hey there, you! You and your buddies! I LOVE you! Always have and always will!

Been missing you, so thought I'd pay a visit. Ya know, you're not that far from my apartment. My DOWNTOWN apartment. I can drive here in about twenty minutes, then walk a mile or so down a wilderness trail to hang with you. To be surrounded by you.

Actually, I should say surrounded by the whole grove of you. 'Cause that's the right word, isn't it? Yeah, you guys make up a grove. You big, beautiful redwood trees, you!

I know you're actually second or third growth, due to your forebears being wiped out a century ago–along with the last of the native people in this area. But you don't give up. I love the way you and your sibs encircle your mom's stump. Your poor dead mom. Or is it your dad? But I worry 'bout you sprouting so close to each other. Don't you know there's not enough room for all of you to hang so near the family roots? Survival of the fittest, we call it.

But I'm honored to meet each of you survivors. At age seventy, I'm a survivor too. And ya know, about forty years ago I lived among some of your cousins up the coast on thirteen acres in Mendocino County. Rather scrawny cousins they were, just fifteen years old and 'bout fifteen feet tall. But they were off to a good start, and during the year I knew them, they grew several feet as they approached adolescence. They must be adults by now. Unless they grew so big during these four decades that the chain saw gang got 'em, just like their parents. That's the problem with you guys. Soon as you grow tall and majestic, with a sturdy, thick torso–er, trunk–you're in danger of being toppled and transformed into deck chairs. Or planter boxes. I wanted to protect your cousins from such an end, but my own life was toppling, so I moved back to the city.

But then, almost twenty-five years later, I found myself once again living among some of your kin in Eureka. Sorry, but it was a LOGGING town. Not on thirteen acres this time, but just half an acre. And these cousins of yours, being young adults already at thirty or forty feet tall, were slated to have a long life. Or so I hoped.

However, one day I heard the screech of death: a chain saw in my neighbor's yard! Indeed, he was maiming your cousins! Not those on my half acre, but the ones who'd had the misfortune to sprout next door. Strangely, my crazed neighbor wasn't sawing into your cousins' trunks near the ground. No, instead of outright killing 'em, he cut their heads off and amputated their needle-laden arms–er, I mean limbs–making 'em look like your forebears who after death were resurrected as telephone poles. When I asked why, he said I should top and de-limb my redwoods too, 'cause in a windstorm they could bend and crack–and fall onto his house. WHAT? I said. My trees aren't going to break apart. I bought this house 'cause I love having redwood trees in my own backyard. I wondered why he'd moved here if he was so prejudiced against your kind.

Unfortunately, I could only keep watch over my little grove–your glorious cousins for a couple of years. Once again, my life began to topple. I had to move away, and I don't know if those relatives of yours survived. My move farther north was to Oregon. Although none of your redwood cousins lives in Eugene, lots of your more distant relations do--especially the Douglas family. The Douglas fir folk, that is. Unfortunately, some hillsides are bare, evidence that the chain saw gang invades Oregon too, but when I lived in Eugene I often visited members of the large Douglas clan on hikes into the Cascades and the coastal range.

Fortunately YOU put down roots in what is now a regional park. No chain saws for you! And I'm so happy to know you're near my city apartment. I promise to visit you often. Since you have a much longer life span than I–actually about three thousand years longer if you manage to avoid the chain saw gang–you're far from even middle- aged. On the other hand, I can't deny that I've entered old age. So when I topple from life the final time (so short by your standards!), I hope my kin will sprinkle my ashes around your trunk.

IT SHOULDN'T HAVE HAPPENED, BUT IT DID
Billie Thompson Bailey

To the memory of those we loved and lost

Too much heartache, too much pain
Too many children who won't see mother and father again
It shouldn't have happened but it did
Too many tears and so much fear
America, oh America, how beautiful you are
Oh America how proud you stand
Let's keep the torch burning
So the haters can see the light
Lord keep us strong so that life can go on
Teach us how to forgive their wrong
It shouldn't have happened but it did
Bless those who lost their loved ones
Let them understand and know you feel their pain
Let them know they shall see them again
In Eternity
It shouldn't have happened but it did
(Peace)

EVERY CLOUD HAS A SILVER LINING
Sreela Banerjee

I volunteer at Richmond Kaiser Hospital two days a week at the front information desk. Our job is to greet everyone who walks through the front door, then help them with their questions and needs.

During these two days I meet lots of people who have various problems, different attitudes and sometimes difficult reactions. Many of them are physically disabled. Our job is to help them with wheelchairs.

Yesterday, while I was there, an Asian gentleman came and asked me if I had change for a dollar. He wanted to make a phone call from the pay phone. I said I could dial the number for him from our desk phone if it was related to the hospital visit. It was, and I made the call. He thanked me and left.

My next job was to take a lady who was in a wheelchair to the second floor. She was extremely heavy and was not in a good mood. Although pushing the chair was hard, I did not have any problem until I tried to get out of the elevator backwards. I had difficulty maneuvering the chair over the slight bump between the elevator door and floor. This really upset her. She yelled at me, "What's the problem?" I said, "No problem. I am just not strong enough."

I couldn't help feeling bad, really bad. There I was, trying to help people on my own, and she treated me like this! But I managed to get over it soon and went on with my work. A few minutes later I saw the Asian gentleman whom I had helped very nominally in the morning. Approaching the desk with a rose in his hand, he said, "If I had more money, I would give you more" and gave the rose as thanks for my help.

The big cloud on my mind from the previous experience now got a shiny bright silver lining! I felt so happy!

(NOT SO) FAR AWAY PLACES
Gilbert Bendix

What were far away places
With strange-sounding names
Are now military bases,
Our colonial domains.

Oh, how many times
Abu Ghraib have I seen
And America's crimes
On my television screen.

Once we couldn't pronounce
Those strange-sounding names;
Now the natives denounce
Us and our fake friendship claims.

May those far away places
Please stay far away;
Close the far away bases
Without any delay.

KNOWLEDGE
Gilbert Bendix

I used to know an awful lot,
Used to.
It isn't just what I forgot,
Oops, no!
So many things that I once knew
No longer happen to be true.

The proton used to be indivisible
And distant galaxies invisible.
That's before quarks and Hubble
Joined to burst my knowledge bubble.
Once butter was considered healthy
And fair-share taxes were paid by the wealthy.

The "facts," that our children now must learn,
Will turn out to be false when it's their turn.

THE GENERAL WISHES ANOTHER HANDWRITING SAMPLE
Ruth Bennett

Funny way to get locked up in jail for a week!

I was a hack poet all my life, a "Reim Dich oder ich fress Dich," – "Rhyme or I'll slurp you up" kind of verse maker am I. I was flipping out verses on the back of envelopes or ad-libbing rhymes in German or English by the yard all my life. I often used a child's name in the middle of a poem when it had a sore tooth maybe, celebrated a birthday, perhaps, or whenever a wedding day, retirement party, the move into a new home or car or such was in the offing, and all the while I had nothing in my head but a little fun. Really, isn't it shocking that somebody ordered: "Lock her up!" for that?

Some folks just don't have a sense of humor.
Honestly, just look at some of my stuff:
It's our loss and we really are sad
It's the saddest good-bye that's ever been said
Who'll direct our songs?
Who'll give us a smile?
Whose kindness will make each new day worth our while? … etc.
Or:
A word is an airplane
A word is a link
A word is a bridge between people
I think.
And though it's oft swollen, just like a carbuncle
It tells what is new betwixt cousin and uncle.
Yet, oft you will meet it all bloody and gory
Right on the front page of a newspaper story. ….etc.

Or perhaps:

Eeny Meeny Miney Mo
Even Mr. Ham has got to go.
To gently retire
And sit by the fire.
I have a suspicion
And my odds are not slim
That th'old rocking chair
Is getting to him………and so on

Or:

We know our gifts you can't take to the banks
We bring appreciation, love, gratitude, thanks.
Our hearts are all filled with esteem and emotion
We respectfully offer our thanks and devotion.

Now what is the harm in that?

German communists of East Germany got me in jail under lock and key right after the war because someone else had written a silly thing making fun of a hefty lady who was running for Lord or Lady Mayor of Langewiesen, and the fat lady thought the poet was me. She wasn't a lady either, and if it wasn't for a bemused general of the Russian army I might sit in the pokey still.

Try to imagine Misters Bush or Gore, Mr. Reagan or any American politician running for office sending the police after someone and incarcerating him or her because he or she made fun of him. Jay Leno beware! "Guard your words, citizens because Big Brother is watching!"

Makes you appreciate the Land of the Free all the more, shortcomings and all.

My story is true.

It's hard to imagine now that my own Langewiesen was occupied by Russian troops after the war, and we were afraid of the Russian soldiers, especially when they had looked into the Vodka glass too deep.

Some of my countrymen became solicitous to the communists. They bowed and scraped and sold their soul, and some women even sold their bodies for a pair of boots, a pound of coffee and the like. But that part you can imagine easily enough.

My nemesis was the strangest of Germans, Frau Storch (Mrs. Stork), a hefty lady barber and I did not even know that she had a beef against me.

Frau Storch had been jailed by Hitler's men during the war, "a political case" as she would have it, and she returned to Langewiesen when the war was over. She was bitter. She didn't seem to have suffered in jail. At any rate she looked very much like a big wrestler and she was not as emaciated as we, the general population, were. Her face was mean as any god-fearing wrestler's, her muscles masculine, her complexion was hale and healthy. She bore a mysterious tattoo on her arm, and I think that to this very day nobody can figure out what that tattoo stood for. It showed three arrows lined up vertically in a row, her "defiance of the Nazis" she would have us believe. We were country bumpkins. Still we know nobody defying the Nazis with three arrows like hers. We don't even have any arrows that I know of.

We think she made up a phantom "freedom party" and by mistake picked an emblem that does not exist.

The Russians used the hammer and sickle on all their stuff. Jews used the Star of David. Germans used the swastika, and you may go around and around the world and never find a tattoo of three arrows in any kind of defiance. *Frau* Storch wanted to be mayor of Langewiesen, and show her clout, and we all sort of avoided her, and sure enough, as my story will show, she fought dirty.

It was two hours past midnight when the communist German secret police pounded at my door. They rifled through my college notebooks and tore out the first page of each, and they arrested me without explanation.

I was driven to a city some 30 miles away, stripped of my purse and shoelaces, and locked in a cell about twelve feet by eight with a window so high up that I had to stand on a high stool to look into the prison courtyard.

Nobody would tell me why I was there and there was no lawyer. It was "political."

Oh, but to be as naïve and innocent again as I was then!

I didn't doubt that everything would be all right, I couldn't remember hurting anyone. Because of this I thought that I just should await justice, and make the best of things in the meantime. I had time on my hands, and I set myself to while it away with the things nobody could take from me and which I love best: I recited poems that I had memorized because they were beautiful, and sang songs of my homeland which I loved…

Goethe was in the hoosegow with me, Shakespeare was there, and Schubert, Mozart, Beethoven, Mörike and Co., and my head was so full of beauty that the first three days passed pleasantly enough. I slept like one with a good conscience, and the bowl of water with a bit of potato and carrot floating inside, my soup, was not much worse than the diet to which the war had acquainted us anyhow. No big deal.

Some uniformed, silent Germans with big boots unlocked my three locks on the fourth day and took me to a lovely mansion and I was "turned over" as political prisoner to "The Russians."

I still had no clue what for.

The piece of drama that followed is worth mentioning.

"The General," a splendid looking Russian man with golden epaulettes on his shoulders sat behind an enormous desk. He held up various pieces of paper like my notebook pages, pointed at them, and bellowed something in a language much more guttural than mine. His Russian voice was deep and beautiful, but I couldn't see what he was showing, I stood too far away.

I told him that I could not understand Russian; an interpreter was summoned and I was somewhat shocked. This was the first time in my life to see a live painted lady, a bilingual one at that. (You know that Russian troops carried their own prostitutes into battle.) So there she was my savior. She told me that "The General" wished to know which ones of the papers I had written.

I asked to approach the desk so I could show him some of my tracts on Fröbel's ideas of how each child follows the evolution of mankind, namely, exploring, roaming, and finally settling at the hearth for which he recommended the ball, the roller, the block for children's earliest toys. That's what the papers from my notebooks were all about–but that wasn't what he wanted to know. I still did not know why I was there but I was soon to figure that out. Funny thing in life is that often times we are forced to be thankful for something we are otherwise ashamed of, and this proved to be one of those times. It was the only time ever that I was overjoyed because my handwriting is pretty doggone awful and virtually unreadable. It was a lark to sort other people's papers from mine when none looked as messy as mine. As I sorted I read some of the others, things I will never forget. Dumb stuff. Dumb poems.

Stuff like:

Horch horch horch	Hark hark hark
Hier wohnt die Frau Storch	Here lives Mrs. Stork
Im K.Z. wurd sie dick und fett	In the pokey she got thick and fat
Jetzt frisst sie unsere Butter weg.	Now she eats our pat of butter yet.

After I was finished with my sorting I looked at "The General" and the General looked up at me. He could easily tell my handwriting from the slur versifiers, and as he looked, fairly close to me now, his expression changed. I saw an intense longing in his eyes. I have seen that look again later in life when a lover went soft. You know the look. That general wasn't nearly as tough as he pretended to be. The man yearned for his wife, I think, or a faraway sweetheart or daughter who must have looked a lot like me. My good stars were ablaze, make no mistake about that.

He turned. He bellowed something in Russian, my two guards grabbed me by the arm, took me back to jail and locked me up again. One finally found his voice and all he said was: "The General wishes another handwriting sample."

They had made a dumb mistake and didn't want to admit it, so they locked me back up. No handwriting sample was ever taken, and they let me go some four days after that.

There was no lawyer, there was no accusation, no explanation, no defense, no apology. I just sat there in my pokey and waited, and while I waited I sang a hundred beautiful songs or more and the jailers released me wordlessly when that was over. They appropriated the money from my purse "for room and board," and returned my shoelaces. I couldn't even ride the train home because my money had gone for water soup with the occasional potato piece and bit of carrot, and for the use of the cell. I partly hitchhiked and partly walked home.

The truckers had very little rationed gasoline and couldn't go more than a mile out of their way, so I only got a friendly short hop here and there, and I left my homeland very soon after that.

During the last four days I had the pleasure of company – another woman prisoner–a thief. I got to be in close proximity and mother confessor to a thief! My heart does not go out to her to this day, but I listened as she unburdened herself. She was sorry but there was nothing to do. She had worked in a sort of storage house in the country where people from big cities had stored furs and such during the war to keep them away from the bombs. She had stolen and sold quite a few fur coats on the black market over the period of about seven years.

The man in the next cell had been her accomplice and they had been caught together. The woman resented being caught. She had lived rather well on black market goods while the rest of us went hungry, but she was ashamed. She remembered with remorse her husband, alas too late. She cried bitter tears when she spoke of him. "Now he will find out. He will never understand. My husband is just a clown in the circus, but he is a good man. A grand man. A great clown. A kind man, and, oh God in heaven, he is an honest man! He will be disappointed in me. Oh, Oh, Oh."

I have sometimes since wondered what became of her and the good clown. I wish him well. I haven't been able to resist the antics of a good clown since childhood. I hope he had a happy life after all that.

The man in the next cell, her friend, paced his cell restlessly all day and all night. I guess it does a soul good to pace, pace, and pace some more when it knows it's done something wrong.

I rapped the rhythm of some of my songs on the wall for him to guess the tune and that calmed him down enough to sleep a while. Sorry, his conscience I could not ease, there was no help for that. I never saw the guy, but I heard him thank me through the wall for his bit of respite.

A good song softens the soul, and as I had always suspected, the hard cot in a jail cell.

I left Langewiesen then, on skis, through my fairylike snowy woods. They decked themselves out in their best for my farewell, – and in the end I came away to live in Texas.

It makes me happy now to think of myself sitting on that cot and singing, singing, and singing of beauty and freedom and of love.

Schiller wrote: "….and if you lock me in the darkest dungeon
>
> You will have failed.
> For my thoughts tear away the bars and chains
> This is true,
> My thoughts remain free."

> *Und sperrt man mich ein*
> *Im finsteren Kerker*
> *Das alles sind rein*
> *Vergebliche Werke.*
> *Denn meine Gedanken*
> *Die reissen die Schranken*
> *Und Ketten entzwei*
> *Es bleibet dabei:*
> *Die Gedanken sind frei.*

Beethoven set this to music. You may have heard it without realizing exactly what it is. The music is as glorious as the words.

Golly days alive! God and the angels themselves provided us with thoughts and songs to lift us above any gloom and doom.

Schiller was right, and I had the privilege to experience it.

I must say it: "Amen."

TO AMERICA
Giovanna Capone

They sent their steamships in droves
eager to scoop up the cheap labor of the Italians
and driven by hunger we fled in numbers
eager to leave our boot-shaped country,
desperate to fill their boats

We came with our saints' faces
our Madonnas and angels
pressed into suitcases
pouring down gangplanks in tattered rags
our pockets empty
our children bedraggled flags behind us
We crept into the depths of steerage
and made a three week voyage over rugged seas
a journey that meant survival

Our boats congested New York Harbor
and Ellis Island exploded with our arrival

As Lady Liberty held her torch
in numbers alone
we altered the course of American history

Filling whole tenements in Little Italy
with sprawling families and clans
we crammed in thick with other *paesani*
One toilet per floor, we lined up even to shit
Our grandmothers never quit scrubbing

the splintered floors of dilapidated buildings
seeking on hands and knees to make them livable
Their wombs pulsed with new life in this new land
so grand with opportunity

Our grandfathers pushed wheel barrows down the city streets
sweeping garbage, shoveling coal, laying bricks
climbing scaffolding like ants
or tunneling like moles to make underground holes
for the subways connecting Manhattan

We also built bridges and roads
toiling in summer heat and winter cold
like Sisyphus in hell
working till New York City swelled
from our backbreaking labor

They sent their steamships in droves
so many years ago
to scoop up the immigrant labor
and driven by hunger, we fled in numbers
to the port cities of Naples and Sicily
eager to leave our boot-shaped country
we were desperate to fill their boats

and the boats congested New York Harbor
and Ellis Island exploded with our arrival

RUSH HOUR IN MANHATTAN
FOR MY SISTER ROSE
Giovanna Capone

At 42nd Street and Grand Central we descend the escalator
joining the mass of humans from every culture
We creep like cattle moving through dingy tunnels and past metal turnstiles
breathing the smell of urine

Green and blue tiles covered with soot spell out "Grand Central Station"
at one time a mosaic of splendid design
Now covered in thick grime

On the platform, waiting for a train,
we see an old lady in a two-toned hat
She sticks her hand out flat and sings in a high falsetto voice
"Help me. I'm hungry."
She sounds like Tiny Tim
But there are no tulips here, no ukuleles to strum
Only the constant hum of subway cars
and the powerful scent of humans

The panicky bleep of a megaphone creaks "Please stand clear of the platform."
Right before the number four closes its doors and speeds off
a homeless man pushes his way through
One more sardine crammed into the pack
His thick and dusty backpack gets trapped in the doors
as the train rushes off, leaving bystanders to gawk

Finally at street level, we trudge through Little Italy
seeking our ethnicity in a plate of food familiar to the tongue
We drink red wine in a cafe
sopping up meat sauce with a crust of bread.
We linger over coffee and biscotti, feeding the Italian back into us
Then stuffed to the gills we pay our bill and leave

Preparing to descend again I hold my nose and wonder
about the ones who actually live under these city streets
in the winter and summer

I think of the guy with the dusty backpack
and my Neapolitan ancestors a hundred years back
who fled here by boat to find a better life

Side by side with millions of others,
they were herded through Ellis Island
just one part of the human tide
a fabric of intricate design composing this land
They were hungry as hell and worked hard to dispel
the grip of poverty choking their lives

Even today, rivers of people still rush to this land
Rushing to be American
they seek freedom and opportunity
the chance for upward mobility
It's the age-old struggle for a better life

But some never make it
They get sent back, hungry and alone
like the Mexicans we call wetbacks
crossing the southwest border, only to be deported
returned to a life of poverty by this land of opportunity.

A few of them get to stay, working gratefully for pennies
America makes good use of its poor.

Going home now, we pass the old lady in the two-toned hat
Her hand is still held out flat and she speaks in a squeaky high voice
Tiny Tim's mother, somebody's mother
Did she ever get something to eat?

A PLACE AT THE TABLE
Giovanna Capone

Growing up Italian American, every Sunday morning my mother would cook a delicious meal always served midday. I have many memories of hearing her rise at six a.m. while the rest of us lingered in sleep, to make and fry her meatballs. In a large bowl, she would blend ground beef, four eggs, seasoned Italian bread crumbs, fresh chopped garlic, and oregano. On that she would sprinkle some grated Parmesan cheese and salt. Then she'd knead the meat till everything was well blended. She would grab handfuls of this seasoned raw meat and in the palms of her hands she'd roll them into spheres about the size of a golf ball. She would lay these meatballs side by side on a flat plate, leaving them to be fried in olive oil a few minutes later.

At this point my mother would begin to make her sauce. She would start by chopping yellow onions, which were lightly sautéed in oil. Some freshly chopped garlic and dried oregano would be added to the onions. Then she would prepare a large pot of tomato sauce. First she would open several big cans of Del Monte tomato puree which had been seasoned to perfection. Next came her sautéed onions and various Italian seasonings, basil and parsley among them. She would be sure to simmer this sauce for a long time. By now she had her meatballs frying in a half inch of olive oil. When they were a crispy dark brown, she would remove them gently, and blot them on a paper towel. One by one she would submerge the plump, round meatballs into her simmering sauce. There they'd sit.

On Sunday my mother always used the same pot, a cavernous stainless steel one. Her sauce would sit simmering and thickening on a burner for several hours. She would stir it occasionally with a wooden spoon. The meatballs would sit in her sauce for just twenty minutes and no longer or they'd fall apart. She added them only for a short while to give her sauce a beefy flavor.

The image of that deep, enormous sauce pot is fixed forever in my mind. The lid was always slightly tipped to allow the steam to escape. In an hour the whole house was flooded with the sweet aroma of my mother's rich tomato sauce quietly bubbling on the kitchen stove.

I have many cherished memories of waking on Sunday morning to the comforting smell of my mother's sauce slowly cooking and the vision of her at work. For hours she'd be in the kitchen, wearing her house slippers, robe, and blue floral print apron, patiently tending her sauce. This memory of my mother cooking still conjures deep feelings of love and security in me that few other experiences in my life will ever match.

Closer to Noon, on a second burner my mother would set a large vat filled with water to boil her macaroni. She would toss in a few tablespoons of olive oil so the pasta wouldn't stick while it was boiling. In minutes the water would be raucously bubbling. Then my mother would ask me to set the table. I usually did so complaining all the while that my brothers never got assigned such a task. Child of the Helen Reddy generation, I didn't see it as a privilege to be the one asked to assist in my mother's ceremony of love. Instead, I would protest about girls' chores, but I would help her anyway.

Regarding family ceremonies, my father had a few of his own. Every Sunday morning he would drive to the local Italian bakery to pick up a fresh loaf of Italian bread. At the newsstand, he'd also pick up a Sunday paper, *The New York Times*. It was thick with advertisements, the crossword puzzle which my mother loved, and the Sunday comics, which I loved. If I woke up early enough, I'd accompany my father on his trip, sometimes selecting the loaf of bread we'd take home. I loved to read the comics on the way home, turning first to *Blondie* and then to *Doonesbury*. The car would be filled with the luscious aroma of the freshly baked bread hiding in its long paper sleeve. I'd be tempted to pick off a few crumbs or a small chunk with golden sesame seeds sprinkled on top. The seeds would accumulate at the bottom of the bag. It was hard to resist breaking off a tasty bite of the crust.

Upon arriving home, my mother would call everyone to the table. We'd rearrange the chairs so we could all sit down in the dining room for a midday meal. Occasionally, we'd open a bottle of red wine. We would consume the familiar food of our culture, eating, sipping wine, talking and laughing through several courses, well into the afternoon.

The pasta, meatballs and sausage would be eaten first, leisurely, and with a chance for seconds. The bread would be on a small wooden carving board on the table. After the pasta and meat, my mother would serve the crispy green salad dressed with olive oil and vinegar in a large white bowl. Black olives in the salad were also one of my favorites and I had to resist picking them out early.

After the salad was eaten, my mother would put a wicker basket of fresh apples, filberts, and walnuts on the table. My father loved to crack open the filberts and pop them into his mouth. With a knife, he'd carve a juicy red apple or two, offering me some, and leaving a tall pile of skins on his plate.

Later, my mother would make a pot of dark coffee and take out some almond biscotti or apple pie. On holidays she usually made her homemade cheesecake with a delicious graham cracker and butter crust. Along with fresh bread, my father would also pick up some freshly baked Italian cookies, or a few chocolate pastries with white or yellow cream oozing from both sides.

This weekend ritual was repeated for our family every Sunday, and on any significant holiday, with my parents both tirelessly contributing their part. As a child, I happily assumed my place in the family mosaic. I loved being part of a big family. Now, as I look back on those bygone Sundays, their memory is even more precious to recall.

Like many young people, at age twenty-two, I was hard-headed and consumed with ideas of my own. I believed I had a mark to make on the world and was eager to make it. So I left New York and my parents' home in a blaze of youthful rebellion, now more than thirty years in the past. Like many other twenty-somethings, I was thrilled to be making my escape. I found a cool job and started working.

I chose to relocate to California, a place I had idealized for years. But despite my huge courage, at that age, I didn't fully realize just how many miles I was actually putting between myself and my family.

Also, I didn't count on the "boomerang effect," a powerful feeling that would hit me hard soon after my departure. In fact, at times it still grips me to this day. By this I mean the unshakeable yearning for family and home with all its elements, one of which was my mother's traditional Sunday meal of sausage, meatballs and macaroni, smothered in a rich tomato sauce as only she could make it.

For many years after leaving New York I began to experience this boomerang effect. It would rebound me back home with a growing force I didn't anticipate. In the years following my departure, I would make regular visits back to New York. On holidays, I flew the long hours in a cramped airplane seat to visit my folks and my siblings, usually arriving on Christmas Eve or New Year's Eve, greeted with hugs and eagerly spilling the latest news and updates from my life in California.

Speaking of California. While living on my own for many years, whenever I made myself dinner the food I always wanted most was pasta. On countless nights in my kitchen it seemed like that was all I ever wanted to eat. Maybe back then it was the only thing I knew how to cook!

In any case I'd prepare a red sauce, frying the yellow onions, throwing in some freshly chopped garlic and oregano, stirring the tomato puree with a wooden spoon and letting it simmer for an hour or more. Then I'd boil my water for spaghetti, or angel hair, or fettuccine, or whatever pasta I desired that night. Whatever kind I chose, it was always pasta I wanted. It was the sweet red taste of tomato sauce that I craved, endlessly, night after night, week after week, month after month, turning my whole life into a series of unending Sunday meals.

Of course, my homemade sauce was never as good as my mother's. As far as fresh bread goes, I found it virtually impossible to find a loaf of Italian bread to match the ones we got from the local Italian bakery in New York.

Even so, for many years I never tired of making my homemade sauce the best I knew how and eating my pasta, especially on Sundays. The sights and sounds of my mother getting up early every Sunday morning had become the mantra for my own Sunday meals. It was a ritual firmly seared into my memory.

Preparing a homemade sauce on Sunday became a ceremony that could soothe me like no other, and in the process my sauce improved too. Of course, today I've also branched out to eat chicken and fish and several other dishes as well, making use of some of the other delicious recipes I witnessed my mother preparing. But as a young person of twenty-something, living three thousand miles away from my family, I felt driven to seek out the food of my culture, the food that nourishes like no other. I needed that food and the Sunday ritual I knew by heart. I loved the vivid memories it conjured of my mother and father, of my Italian American culture, and of the warmth and security they tirelessly recreated for our family.

For me, cooking on Sunday will always conjure a magical feeling. I have internalized a composite image of my family mosaic. It's a deeply personal and enduring image, and enormously comforting regardless of what else is happening in my life. In this image I will always see myself and I will always play an active role. I belong to a family with longstanding roots, and I love that.

Today at fifty-two, making and eating macaroni has remained evocative for me. I'm grateful for those early rituals of my parents and still find them satisfying even as an older adult. I still need to feel my parents' nurturing hands the capable hands of my father driving us home; and the loving hands of my mother frozen in time stirring her sauce on Sunday mornings. Perhaps my own rituals are an attempt to convince myself that in effect I never left home because home is now a place deep inside me.

With both of my parents now gone and my family spread miles apart, it's up to me to create feelings of family and home. I do this best with food and most often on Sundays, keeping alive aspects of my culture that I inherited and learned from my constant observation as a child.

With the focused efforts of my own hands in my own kitchen, I conjure a place at the table. I'm lucky to have these rich and longstanding traditions. I renew them whenever I want to in my own way, in my own time, despite the fewer settings at my table.

MY REFLECTION IN THE POND
Gere Cherry

What is it that I see when I see my reflection in the pond, as opposed to what I see when I look at myself in the mirror? It's something about the reflection in the pond that stirs something deep in my soul. Fragments of a life lived, as best served by your memories of those experiences.

It's like a mosaic–the pieces of colored glass bound in cement, forming a picture of all the things, places and people who have influenced my life, cemented in my soul. The mosaic is lasting and has meaning to the person who creates such a beautiful work of art. I am God's work of art.

The reflection in the pond is not static, but is fluid and moving and changing like life and me. That moving reflection captures my life experiences. A piece represents my grandparents' home in Hartshorne, Oklahoma, and the smell of my grandfather's Doc Martins. He is cooking a breakfast of bacon, sausage links, scrambled eggs, and oatmeal. Umm, the smell of fresh coffee brewing at 5:00 a.m. That's one of the reasons I am an early riser. My grandfather loved to cook and he was skilled at using his cast iron skillets to create the most tender and delicious roast in a mushroom gravy, mashed potatoes and fresh green beans with ham hocks. I have memories of our family sitting together at the table and talking and sharing what we all had experienced that day; thanking God, and being grateful for having what we had.

How special you feel being part of a family. Most of all, eating such a delicious meal prepared by the kindest person who loved his family very much.

Those memories are a part of who I see in the reflection in the pond. It's the caring me that I unconditionally share with my family and my friends, or even strangers. Then there is the private me who longs for solitude from the fast moving pace of life and its many demands on your time and energy. I am a wife, mother, sister, auntie, grandmother, and most importantly, I'm me, myself and I.

Another piece of the mosaic are the teachers who influenced my appreciation for learning. Mrs. Johnston, my high school music teacher, taught me the appreciation for all kinds of music. I have learned to embrace hip hop and rap. My daughter thinks this is weird for my age. Geraldine Little, my middle school English teacher, taught me the importance of learning to spell. Mrs. Herzer, my high school English teacher, allowed me to express myself through writing. This was the beginning of a lifelong passion.

My uncle, Douglas Coleman, pushed me to fulfill my lifelong dream of writing and having my work published. I am very grateful that he saw the potential and encouraged me to write. I didn't think what I had to say was relevant, but he proved me wrong. His

wife, my aunt Arlene, is my mom's baby sister. She has been just as instrumental in helping fulfill my dream. She had my last story published in our hometown newspaper. This is another jewel that adds to my life experience.

I feel happy and safe when I travel back in time through my memories– it feels like it was a moment ago, but it was as lifetime ago. I remember walking with my friend to Hartshone Lake. I can still feel looking up at the beautiful clear blue sky with white fluffy clouds and the hot sun turning already dark skin even darker. My hometown was a small country town, but I feel the people's caring and sharing spirit helped shape much more of who I am than I really understood.

I reside in San Mateo, California, and have been here for forty years. It is hard to imagine that I have been in one place so long. People are always saying how nice I am. I would jokingly say that I was taught that by the kindness of the many people I grew up and interacted with back in my home town.

The people you share your life with, or extend a helping hand to, or anyone who asks without having to question the reason you are being asked to help, are the bits and pieces of your life's mosaic.

Through technology and travel, the world can now be easily accessed. Living in a fast- paced world has taught me to slow down, and to appreciate and love myself just as I am with all of my imperfections. All the tiny pieces and experiences have come to form the most beautiful mosaic of a life well lived and shared with many wonderful people.

FEAR OF LIVING
Pearl Chinn

In an earthquake
being buried alive,
suffering from thirst
and hunger,
unable to move
because of injuries,
> I would be fearful of living.
> I'd rather be dead.

Living to a ripe old age
is fine
as long as I am able
to care for myself
and have all
my faculties.
To be dependent on others
to feed me
and change my diapers,
> I would be fearful of living.
> I'd rather be dead.

To be blind
and live in darkness,
to be deaf
and live in silence,
> I would be fearful of living.
> I'd rather be dead.

Do we have a choice
or should we have a choice
of living
or dying?
> This is a dilemma
> facing all humankind.

PLACES TO SLEEP
Pearl Chinn

Because of crowded conditions at home in the 1940s in San Francisco, my sister and I benefited from the generosity of others by making use of space temporarily vacated by men who were drafted. First, my sister and I went to stay overnight at my aunt's apartment three blocks away. Auntie Woo was my mother's sister. The Woo's only son was drafted into the U.S. Army so his room was empty. We only went there to sleep. In the morning Auntie Woo would fry an egg and the three of us shared it with some leftover rice for our breakfast. It was generous of her to share her breakfast with us.

The second place we stayed was with a widowed neighbor in the south side of the apartment house where we lived. Her two sons were also drafted into the U.S. Army so she had an empty room, where my sister and I stayed. She had a sofa bed in her living room that opened up to sleep two people.

I remember a strange experience while sleeping there. One day in the early morning, I was awakened suddenly and I found I couldn't move. I was paralyzed. I tried to scream but no sound came out. I was fully awake and was not dreaming. I sensed a presence in the room as if someone was watching me, but I couldn't see or hear anything. I was afraid and didn't know what to think. This lasted for several long minutes, and then it was over. This happened one other time when I stayed at that apartment. My sister who slept right next to me on the sofa didn't feel or hear anything. My mother told me she had a similar experience sometime in her life. She told me that the Chinese believe it was a ghost leaning against me. I am still puzzled over this. Sixty-five years have passed and I can still recall the incidents as if they had happened yesterday.

Another experience I had when I was a teenager: I was at San Francisco General Hospital having a tonsillectomy. I was given an anesthetic and before long I had an out-of-body experience. I was out of my body and looking down on myself on the operating table. Soon I was roaming around the hospital observing all that was going on. My mind was very clear. It was as if there were no unanswered questions. All was clarity and there was a sense of peace and well-being. This lasted only several minutes and it was over.

Because of these experiences I do believe that there is another level of consciousness, and there is a life hereafter. There are so many things we don't understand. We can only live by faith, living a life worthy of God's calling, and hope in the end there will be a reward in Heaven.

THE INTERPLAY OF WORDS:
Raymond Chow

The Beauty of Words
Incubating in the womb – of my mind
Nurturing in the reservoir of words –
Developing – gestating –
To birth of poetic lines.

The Interplay of Words,
There permutation is infinite.
Poets extrapolate Words
Into metaphors – similes – idioms –
Structured sources
For prose and poems.

Bouncing words on cranium wall
Rebounding opposing words off wall,
Flip it – flop it – spin it around
Till it quenches – the thirst for words.

The Interplay of Words,
Listen – listen to your inner voice
For euphonious Words
For harmonic convergence
Of sounds – rhythms – and rhymes –
That dances in the chasm of your mind
And as palatable as wine.

The Interplay of Words
Words that resonate
And stir the depth of minds.
The power of Words
Those wondrous Words
Explode on empty pages
Imploding in the mind
Evoking transcendental imagery
That touches – the palate of minds.
Imagery – is the Heart and Soul of Poetry.

The aesthetics of punctuation is nil
As it floats over written lines
Integrating where it's needed
And ends this poem –
With the final period.

I FOUND MY INNER PEACE
Raymond Chow

I yearn to find that inner peace.
My endearing love for my granddaughters
The things they say or do
From the sublime to unmentionable.
Spontaneous – unrehearsed –
'Tutu U got We-We?'
'My Da-Da got We-We.'
Momentary shock! –
State of denial! –
Burst of EXUBERANT LAUGHTER –
Titillating my funny bone to the core –
Medication for my aging soul.

Rivulets of curls flow below her shoulders
Framing her milky white face.
Sparkling round eyes –
Peek thru curtain of frizzy curly-locks –
Staring up with a smile.
Her pink lips spread out like wings –
Of an angel ready to take flight.
'Tutu U Da Bess!'
Our connection – and bond will last and last.
KEALOHA MO'OPUNA KEIKI WAHINE.
I FOUND MY INNER PEACE.

Tutu means Grandpa
KEALOHA MO'OPUNA KEIKI WAHINE is a Hawaiian phrase,
and it means means love of little granddaughter

RESTORATION OF FAITH WITH MANKIND
Raymond Chow

Inner voices of anger:
Saber rattling – pestilence of wars
The slaughter of 4 Oakland Police Officers
Drive-by shootings of innocent casualties
Foreclosures – homelessness
Crumbling infrastructure
Diminishes my faith with mankind.

Mired in traffic at critical hour of madness –
in midst of maelstrom of road rage –
cacophony of horns blaring in anger –
entombed in sarcophagus of my car –
claustrophobia –
sounds beyond decibel of tolerance –
confused – in quandary of hopelessness –
paranoia sets in – what to do?
Two strangers – Hispanic and White
attempted to unplug the bottleneck.
Asian Police officer wave-off Good Samaritans
patrol-car tucked me into pocket of safety.

There is goodness in our citizens of Milpitas –
in times of economic down-turn –
people are drawn together
for the common good for all.
Our citizens have so little to give –
they gave themselves
to aid a little old confused man.

In midst of maelstrom –
the goodness of mankind
displaces anger.
Restoration of faith with mankind.

THE YEARNING HEART
Douglas E. Coleman

Oh Yearning Heart
Pulsating Mind
Calm thyself
Restore thy Balance

Embrace Truth
That barometer
For distinctions
Since The First Time

Oh Bringer into Being
Don't let the crocodiles drag the people away

The water's edge is far away
Yet the predators strike
The people cry out
In pain and suffering

But the turned away face
Where indifference prevails
With salivating jaws dripping
With capitalist possibilities

Oh Beneficent One
Don't let the crocodiles drag the people away

Air is to the nostrils
As water is to roots
Nourishing
Sharing the essence

Inhalation brings Life
Air filled lungs
Steady heart beat
Sight, Touch, Brain yields Mind

Oh One Mind!
Don't let the crocodiles drag the people away

THE TROUBLING OCEANS
Douglas E. Coleman

The old man looked longingly out over the white-sand beach toward the massive waters of the Atlantic Ocean. He sat alone at his favorite table at the Beach Man Bar & Restaurant with its bright color of gold with red and green trim. The local flora of philodendrons, palms and spices were all aromatic and aesthetically pleasing. A folded copy of *The New York Times* lay on the right side of the table. A portion of the headline was still visible. The visible portion of the headline read ...*Another Shark Attack!* The old man used both of his rough and scarred hands to sip his favorite Jamaican Blue Mountain coffee. He sipped from a large ceramic mug. The coffee was hot, black and rich the way he liked it. He sipped and savored the rich brew without additives. He loved the taste of the coffee bean alone. His dark skin bore the impact of long hours under the sun and more than forty years at sea–thirty years as a merchant seaman, and ten as a commercial fisherman. He loved the oceans, mourned their demise, but at this moment he would not go near the oceans.

The ocean's waters around the southern tip of Florida appeared as beautiful as ever. The clarity of the water could be seen at depths of thirty feet and beyond. Diverse and multi-colored sea plants lent a colorful and pleasing effect from above or below the surface. The warm tide waters gently washed the white-sand beaches to and fro, as a promise of peace and tranquility. The sky above was light blue and clear from horizon to horizon. The sky was clear with a large number of sea gulls and other sea birds over the waters, feeding at will. A year ago the beach would have been filled with tourists and locals. The beach goers would be sun-bathing, swimming and frolicking in the waters. The infectious island music of salsa, reggae, soca and merengue, would be blaring unending from vendors' shops, but today there was no one on the beach and no music came from the empty vendors' shops. The old man furrowed his brow, sipped his coffee and allowed his mind to reflect on when it all began. When did it begin? Who could say for sure? He had studied and followed the impact of ocean pollution for over thirty years as a merchant seaman and commercial fisherman. He had witnessed changes unfold before his very eyes in the dumping and harvesting of the oceans. He concluded, as others, that the Industrial Revolution was a strong contributor to our current crisis. Some say that the Industrial Revolution brought about many positive societal changes in housing, manufacturing, transportation, communication and production. The old man mused that the Industrial Revolution had brought about some negative factors as well. Humans have been fishing and traveling the oceans for thousands of years. After the introduction of industrialization to European societies–around 1760 and later to much of the world–we find after approximately 250 years, the oceans of Earth are nearly inaccessible to humans.

On a Monday afternoon about a year ago, a small shrimp boat captain named Jared Miles spoke from the deck of his battered shrimp boat to the local media in Miami, Florida. He spoke about the crew and his horrifying ordeal at sea. Mr. Miles filed a formal report with the Florida Coast Guard whereby he stated the same as he did before the local TV stations. He stated emphatically that the shrimp boat, crew and he were attacked by a large whale shark. The whale shark appeared to weigh over two tons, and was more than thirty feet long. Choking up at times, Mr. Miles recounted how the whale shark seemed angry and keenly focused on the attack. He spoke of how again and again the whale shark slammed its massive body against the forty-foot shrimp boat. Crewmen on the boat said that the animal came high out of the water, its eyes fixed on the crewmen and its giant mouth of razor-sharp teeth snapping like an enraged pit bull. The attack had lasted for several minutes before the bloody animal continued on its way. The pictures of the battered shrimp boat showed severe damage. Two crewmen received broken arms while another had a concussion and a torn ear. The Coast Guard sent ships and helicopters to the area and surrounding waters, but no sight of the whale shark was seen. Two weeks after the Jared Miles incident three hammer-head sharks attacked swimmers at a beach in Miami. Several swimmers received serious bites and lashes to their legs, but fortunately no one died. Hammer-head sharks are not perceived as aggressive. One month to the day of the attack on Miles' shrimp boat, a thirty-foot cabin cruiser was attacked and sunk by a single whale shark. All aboard, including the owner, his wife and a couple, were lost. Before the cruiser went down the owner, Stanley Harrington, was able to get an emergency call out. Two vessels, another cabin cruiser and a Florida Coast Guard ship received the call and both captains confirmed that Harrington stated that "… they were under attack from a large fish that looked like a large shark." Mr. Harrington was reporting the animal's vicious assault on his cruiser and how he had "looked into the eyes of the beast" when the transmission went silent.

Soon there were reports from around the world of sea animals acting strangely and attacking people at sea and on beaches. There were reports of giant squid and octopus attacking people. These reports were of particular concern since these creatures live primarily in the deep waters of the oceans. The report of octopus attacks came when a forty-foot cabin cruiser was attacked. The cruiser was about to dock at a local port in the state of Washington. Witnesses reported seeing three long tentacles extend out of the water and drape across the deck of the cruiser. The huge tentacles swept the three occupants from the deck and their bodies were never recovered.

Killer whales traveling in packs attacked a large yacht and killed most of the passengers. The survivors of the attack on the yacht remain deeply traumatized. There were several reports of large Blue Gills and Sail Fish crashing onto the deck of fishing boats, injuring crewmen then returning to sea. Some crewmen on the boats were injured, and in one instance a man was killed.

It was apparent that humans were no longer safe on the seas and beaches. The animals of the sea were turning on humans with a viciousness never seen before. It seemed that any time individuals or a vessel forty feet or less was at sea they were at increased risk for attacks. The attacks came primarily from the whales and sharks. All species of whales and sharks carried the attacks, from the peaceful Pilot Whales to the packs of Killer Whales. From the Hammer-head sharks to the Great Whites, these animals went on the attack against humans in the water and in their lesser vessels on the seas. During these attacks on vessels, the animals would damage themselves to a bloody mess, as if impervious to pain and driven by a desire greater than self-preservation. The torn and lost body parts from these encounters provided ample food for sea birds and fish.

The old man accepted a refill of the steaming brew from a young waitress whom he did not know. It had been six months since several federal and private agencies agreed that there was a problem with the sea animals. The source of the problem was believed to be something in the oceans' waters. That something was making the large sea animals angry, unpredictable and aggressive. The general public was advised to stay out of the waters and those with boats to stay close to the shores. Cargo ships were advised to travel in convoys with Navy battle ships as escorts. Various agencies were doing research on the recovered dead bodies of sharks and whales.

Returning his attention to *The New York Times* article, the one that stated that after six months of study and analysis The Society of Oceanography had concluded that the behavior of the whales and sharks was caused by a new marine organism, Tetraleoceanism. The microscopic organism attaches to the base of the brain of these animals. From there the organism multiplies and slowly destroys the brain tissue of its victim as it grows. During the organism's growth the animals grow aggressive and are slowly driven mad. The article went on to state that the scientists of The Society of Oceanography believe the organisms developed from the accumulated amounts of lead, toxins and industrial waste in the oceans. This pollution, along with the increased salinity of the oceans and the steady warming of the oceans' waters gave rise to the new organism.

The old man sighed as he read that the oceanography people, nor any of their colleagues, knew how the organism could be eradicated. They did not know how the sharks and whales could be handled or cured. They mentioned that the organism had been found in smaller fish as well. This could mean that predatory fish, such as sharks and killer whales, could receive an increased exposure to the organism. Other articles reported that the world's fishing industries were destroyed. Fishermen were not safe on the seas. Cargo routes were altered to lessen or avoid confrontation with attacking sea animals. Popular beaches that once offered great surfing, snorkeling and sun bathing were now deserted. Cruise ship sat idle at docks with few people venturing onto the oceans. International economies were being devastated by their inability to conduct business on the seas or at the sea's edge. The heads of nations, their top scientists in the fields of oceanography and their top naval officers, were gathering at The Hague to devise strategy. Unemployment had climbed to 16 % and threatens to go higher. It didn't take long for national and international anger and accusations to gain momentum. Some of the anger came from environmental groups that charged the International Corporations and their boards as the primary agents of the "reckless thrust of industrialization." Numerous critics charged that 80% of the ocean's pollution was due to human activity of more than 300 years of dumping into the oceans of Earth. In the dumping of industry and manufacturing waste, they point to mining, oil production, and medical waste as leaders in the dumping-pollution practices. Modern technology joins the practice with its use of components that emit low levels of radiation and toxicity. Industry, manufacturing, technology and common household waste eventually end up in our oceans in some portion.

Supporters of industrialization, and its aggressive thrust, claimed that conceptual advancements and modern technology brought on by industrialization would find an answer to the problem of the marine organism. They cautioned that there was still time to reverse this event. They offered no concise ideas or action. Their current efforts were focused on finding a way to eradicate the marine organism, Tetraleoceanism, that was infecting the large sea animals. The advocates for continued and increased industrialization said that the best minds in the world on oceanography, marine life and bio-pharmacology were working on the problem. That it was just a matter of time before and answer would be found. Would they be successful? The old man did not know. He hoped that they would. He drained the last of his coffee, left his customary tip, picked up his copy of *The New York Times* and walked out. He walked away from the ocean with a kind of finality. He walked with his back straight, using wide strides. He never looked back in full recognition that life on Earth was about to take a new and dramatic turn. Would humanity survive? Would he survive it? Who knew?

UNTITLED
Ken Coleman

We are the dust of stars
Holding the heartbeat of the universe

At constant
We are the sands of time
Where dreams are channeled
And hopes are cast upon the waves

Of feeling
We cannot visualize darkness
In the sublime absence of light
Where truth, as change, is inevitable
We cannot know light
When our candles are without wick

We are the sequence of all possibilities
Grounded in the blink of satisfied
Human frailty…
We always begin
We always end
Circles have no centers
And gods??

Gods are the fear of self.

FINGER PRINTS AT A NAZI PRIMARY
Cynthia Drori

I a woman in a room,
A shut door;
Is it closed? Is it locked?
Plays the pen and the flute—
Windows stay on my mind
Why was it who was singing of this?

Perfume, flowers,
red wrapping tissue,
A gold diadem.

Perfume sings on my mind;
Passing the window a donkey cart drives,
Who is in it? Driving?
Plays the pen and flute;
Is this justice please?

Outside the window a donkey cart drives
in the opposite direction
Justice is an explanation,
This time, the cart refuses to stop.
This is a disguised route of cart and bull.

Who blows it? in the wind?
The donkey cart is hard to take.
Example of expelling and escape.
Cart and bull stays on my mind.
The excuse is Humphrey.

Justice plays with my mind.
Looking on the diaphragm—
Looking out of the window;
Do I play the flute?
The pen,

Episcopal for itself. Explains to me,
The reason for your cart and pony.

Whomever you were when I saw you outside?
This very window,
For example, leading my cart
With a pony;
The example of explaining –
The cart,
The pony,
My justice - of writing for flute?

A visionary episode
Of the street outside my window
For example: why do I see you?
Because you are within my vision—
But what is outside?
Nothing but space, the outside—
The space where you make work with my pony.

THE SALUBRIOUS SEA
Marilyn Dumesnil

I left her in the beach house, sitting on the window seat,
afternoon sun streaming in, warming her as she watched
wave after wave bombard the sand, sending puffs of foam
across the beach, like lacey blowing snow.
Walking heated sands, in a moving meditation, I carry her with me.
On sand, where she hasn't the strength to walk, I walk.
Wishing her health, I walk, healing her damaged lung.
Calling on the power that controls the waves, controls the tides,
I beg, "Hold back the wave ravishing her body."
Reaching out to the supreme healer, mother, father of us all,
I plead for the return of her fine gold tresses, her crown.
Wrapping up all my anger and fear, I imagine it tied in a burlap bag,
and tossing it to the ebbing tide, it floats out to sea.
Who is that on the lookout bench, her hat a shade from October's sun?
Where does she find the muscle to move amidst exhaustion?
Joyfully, I climb the dunes to join her.
Then before sitting ask, "Would you rather be alone?"
"No, sit" she answers. And so I do.
In silence our thoughts combine, go arm in arm.
Then after a moment, peace pervades.
And then it's only sand and sea, the crash of waves, the call of gulls,
the salt air breeze, and I and she.

WHY I STOPPED SMOKING
Lucy Ely

I remember when I was a girl of eleven or twelve, my brother and sister and I would practice smoking. We would use dried leaves wrapped in old paper bags. Sometimes we would smoke under the house or sometimes out in the toilet. Old southern homes were built up high off the ground. We could see someone coming before they saw us.

We had just finished washing and hanging out two lines of clothes. Mother and Daddy decided to go fishing. The fishing creek was about three miles from the house. Mother and Daddy had to walk, so we knew we had lots of time. My brother decided we would use fig leaves this time. We decided we would smoke three cigarettes apiece.

While my brother and sisters prepared the cigarettes I went to the kitchen to get some matches from the box Mother kept in a cabinet. We decided not to hide because we had lots of time. So we sat under the clotheslines and smoked and laughed. Suddenly we looked up and saw our neighbor's car coming down the road with Mother and Daddy in it. We didn't know what to do. My brother grabbed all our cigarettes and hastily stuffed them in the back pocket of Daddy's overalls that were hanging on the line. Then we ran into the house and got under the bed. All of a sudden the overalls caught on fire and two lines of clothes went up in flames. Daddy and our neighbor put out the fire before it got to the house, but all the clothes and bedding were lost. Mother whipped us all soundly and on that day I decided to give up smoking.

MAMA WON'T YOU PLAY FOR ME JUST ONE MORE TIME
Carol L. Evans

You told me how you learned to play in your home town
I haven't heard you play since I was a small child
Back then, it just was not enough for tiny ears to hear
The sound of your music, I barely remember those years
Mama won't you play for me --- just one more time

Nobody knows anymore the music you played for me
Few families even know and others can't recall
That music was part of your life, years long before
I know that it was taught to you, all your young life
Mama won't you play for me --- just one more time

I never saw enough of you on that piano stool
You were the master over those ivory keys
You learned to play – Bach, Beethoven and Chopin
This should never be forgotten or lost from our mind
Mama won't you play for me --- just one more time

We know sometimes life gets in the way
And that's why you could not continue to play
Those who don't believe, never heard your music
Will be convinced by me, how well you touched those keys
Mama won't you play for me --- just one more time

The music you learned to play, so beautiful to be near
And you also mastered your studies during those years
Earned your membership in the National Honor Society
For all those who do not know, I have proof of that to show
Mama won't you play for me --- just one more time

Your music mattered so much you had it taught to us
We now understand how life sometime gets in the way
Sadly enough, the music you loved so much stopped with us
But that is not a reason to forget ---- So
Mama won't you play for me --- just one more time
Please Mama please

RETURNING HOME ON THE CALIFORNIA ZEPHYR
Carol L. Evans

My last day in California was over at a friend's home, sharing memories and coming to the realization of soon living thousands of miles apart. That evening, she hosted a lovely party for me and many of our friends – to say goodbyes. Many of these guests had attended another party given for me two weeks earlier, by a long-time friend.

The following morning, my friend drove me to the train station. We hugged and shared expressions of "best wishes" for our futures. Because of her insatiable spirit of adventure, we traveled the world. I learned how fascinating, old, and beautiful our world is, "thanks" to her. This friend turned what could have been an untraveled existence into a life of adventure and learning, which continues to this day. We now take shorter trips and stay closer or within the U.S.

I went inside the train station to complete my final ticket arrangements. I found a seat and waited for the arrival of the California Zephyr. After 36 years, I am returning to where I call home. After all the years in California, it was never like home – especially in the fall and Christmas.

I had packed two journals for this trip to make sure thoughts and feeling would be recorded. Memories of my years in California with family and friends are important to me.

But getting to know all the "greats"–nieces and nephews–in my sister's family, continuing my writing, and growing old gracefully, is now my paramount goal.

Before long, I heard my train announcement. I collected all my belongings, stepped outside on this heavenly day and started walking next to the tracks – watching my train approach. I listened to the familiar rumbling and screeching sound of steel on the tracks and that famous whistle announcing its arrival.

My heart beat with excitement about the prospect of returning to my roots, and starting a new life. After all these years, I knew I just couldn't pick up where my life had left off. So many of my friends were deceased and others had evolved into people I hardly recognized as once being my friends. We were no longer children and traveled different life journeys. But I knew I could settle down and just start doing whatever I needed to do without any fear.

After my train stopped, a line began to form. I overheard someone say, "This line is for first class passengers." I was grateful to receive the gift of a "first class" ticket for my return home. I watched a train attendant approach us – calling my name. I was startled, but quickly composed myself and held up my hand. "Please come with me," she said. "My name is Kathy. I will be your attendant, all the way to Chicago." Then reaching for my luggage, she led the way to the next train car.

She was a tall, big-boned woman, with short blond hair poking out from underneath her blue train cap. She wore a dark blue uniform over a starched white blouse, with a small blue tie. As I ascended the train steps, she talked about her responsibilities and my location on the train.

After entering my compartment, she showed me how the sofa turned into a bed. (There was also an overhead bed.) She would check with me in the evenings and mornings – just buzz her when I wanted my bed made. She continued showing me where things were and how to use different gadgets that would make my life comfortable for the next three days.

There was an armchair, small table that hung from the wall, or could be pushed up when not in use, a full-length mirror, and my toilet and shower. There was a small sink with a mirror above, and cabinet space underneath that held extra towels. I also had a small closet with three hangers. She showed me where the coffee, tea, juices, and rolls were, near my compartment.

I was given the hours for service in the diner and information about other train amenities. The attendant excused herself and closed my door.

After becoming familiar with my surroundings and finding convenient places for my belongings, I discovered the great view from a large window in my compartment. If I left the curtain, in front of my door, pulled back, I could see through the windows directly across the aisle. I didn't want to miss the picture perfect view of the San Francisco skyline, the Golden Gate Bridge, and the imposing view of the Bay.

The observation cars have glass bubble roofs and you have a panoramic view of the mountains. The observation cars offer a chance to meet and talk with other travelers. The seats are designed to swivel and show a full view from any positions. There are tables nearby for refreshments. The first night I retired early too much excitement!

The next morning I had breakfast brought to my compartment. I might as well test the service! I was excited about my first full day on the train. I loved walking through the train cars, rocking side to side, and taking cautious steps to balance myself while pushing open the sliding doors between the cars, then walking past the many riders on my way to the dining car for my lunch. I always loved going there for meals. The first things you notice are tables, along both sides of the car, covered with white table cloths and floral center pieces on each table. You are met at the door by the dining car attendant. "Good afternoon, Madam. How many, please?" I answered, "Good afternoon, one, please." The attendant led me to a table, helped me with my chair, handed me a menu and said "your waiter will be right here." I responded with a smile. The view is always perfect from any table and the service and food is especially good.

For the rest of my trip, I kept occupied in and out of my compartment enjoying and exploring my surroundings, speaking to travelers throughout the train, calling my friends and family with updates on my whereabouts, writing "Thank You" notes for gifts and heartfelt words from all the friends who attended the parties given for me. I was coming home with lots of optimism about my future.

I looked out my window at the rear of the train, slowly curving around the tracks and climbing past huge rocks. I went to the observation car to witness nature; we were in Colorado. The scenery was magnificent as we followed the Colorado River. Suddenly there were mountains resembling red clay, with greenery protruding through. Sandy dry spots appeared and disappeared into the Colorado River.

Clear, quiet water slowly rippled over rocks, in deep gorges. Nature is a perfect landscaper.

Our first stop was Grand Junction, Colorado. The mountain air was wonderful. We were able to disembark, do a little shopping at the general store, and then continue on our way to Chicago. We were running eight hours behind. Once we left Colorado, our train was able to make up some of the lost time.

Back in my compartment, I stared out the window and my mind drifted back to my first plan for retirement. It wasn't the "coming home plan." I thought about how close I came to living out my dream to live in Mexico, in an American retirement community. I remember the first time I laid eyes on that place. I never imagined such a piece of paradise existed within my reach.

This was going to be my paradise on earth, hidden away from everything I wanted to leave behind. I just wanted to be left alone to reach the end of my journey, in peace. This beautiful place between the majestic red clay mountains and the Sea of Cortez, about three hours from San Diego, would bring peace of mind and serenity to my soul, I so badly sought.

I purchased a lovely corner lot with flowering cactus plants that would surround the house I would build. I paid faithfully on my land with dreams of a brightly colored stucco house, with a veranda, beautifully tiled floors, tiled walls in the kitchen and bathrooms. The house would have lots of windows and open spaces with views of the majestic mountains and hundreds of blooming and flowering cactus plants. This was going to be my retirement dream come true.

The community around my land was a bustling, growing place with many American families living out their dreams. How I envied them – this was what I also wanted. I wanted to live among all this beauty, peace, wonderful amenities and resources this American retirement community would provide. The white sandy beaches, with many water sports, restaurants, a spa, golf course, exercise facilities and much, much, more. This was all next to a tiny, sleepy Mexican town with lots of shops and restaurants. Also, a small well-equipped hospital and clinic was nearby. But the down turn in the California housing market foiled my dream.

I picked up my journal and started to write down my memories. That's all I had left of my paradise. Now I'm going farther away than I ever thought I would be from my paradise – traveling east. There must be another plan I know nothing about?

That night, I was awakened by the roar of the engines, the train whistle, and the side to side rocking from the speed of the train. We were out of the mountains. I didn't sleep well that night. I kept peeping out my window, admiring the star-filled sky, and trying to recognize images from the light of a full moon. I didn't regret choosing the train over the airplane. I accomplished much. I had time to think and contemplate what I wanted to put on my "Bucket List."

The next morning I awakened to gaze at cornfields, John Deere billboards, white farm houses, red barns, silos and grazing cows. What a difference a few days make! Tonight we would arrive in Chicago, only six hours late, and missing my connection. I will be a little sad to leave the train and all the wonderful memories. I was remembering the friendly lady from Utah I met and invited to visit with me in my compartment. She was traveling for the first time on a train and had not been in the compartments. There was also that good looking, young couple from Florida I met in the upper lounge and had drinks with, while we tried to solve all the problems of the world.

It was time to start tidying up things and organizing my packing. Soon the attendant came to my compartment announcing our arrival. Late that night, I disembarked from the train and had to be rushed, by one of the station attendants, to my bus. After a four-hour bus ride from Chicago, I arrived safely in Indianapolis at 3:00 a.m. I was very tired, but delighted to be greeted lovingly by my very sleepy and smiling sister. She had come alone. The marching band and the "Welcome Back Home" signs had not arrived.

THE TRAVELING HEART
Carol L. Evans

Many years ago there was a middle-age gentleman who was a magnificent writer. He became famous in his hometown because everyone who knew him often heard the stories of the "love letters" to a lady living far away.

Because of his superb knowledge of the English language, during his time in the military he often received requests from the men in his unit to write love letters for them. These letters were mailed to their sweethearts. Jake was flattered and proud to be of assistance in helping love travel so far.

Jake Heart had lived all his life in the town of Wasilla, Maine, where he worked at the post office for many years. Wasilla's population was 896. Its industries were fishing and tourism. During the summer its harbor was always a busy place, filled with small fishing boats, sail boats, and a few expensive yachts. During the summer months, the yachts were a beautiful sight to watch coming around the bend – in and out of the harbor. Some of the wealthier families sailed to Wasilla on their way to their summer homes. They would moor their boats and shop at the businesses along the wharf.

Jake would frequent the barber shops, cafes and the general store, telling his stories about the lady he loved so much, and hoped they would soon be together. Folks always asked him how many letters he had written in the past months, and if he and his lady friend would soon marry. Jake had never married and he was always teased by everyone about needing someone to cuddle up with during those cold winter nights in Maine. His only companion was a 15-year-old black and white cocker spaniel named Joe. Jake and Joe were a constant fixture on the streets of Wasilla and down by the harbor they loved so much.

Jake would always promise that his lady friend would visit soon, and then everyone would have a chance to meet her and see how beautiful and kind she was. But months and months, and years and years went by. Jake's lady friend and love never arrived. Jake had often said she was afraid of flying, and the train or bus was such a long ride, Jake often traveled to visit her.

Some of his friends noticed that Jake seemed to be having a few health challenges. They worried because he was alone and was not close to any of his relatives. One day while he was having his hair cut, his barber became concerned about how weak he seemed to be. Jake had never complained or mentioned any illness. He left the shop with old Joe and slowly made his way home.

Folks began to see less and less of Jake and his dog. And since he retired from the post office, he was hardly ever seen except when he was mailing his love letters or doing a little shopping. Then one day neighbors noticed the ambulance, police and fire truck in front of Jake's house. Neighbors watched while Jake was carried out and put into the ambulance. The next day when his friends received the news of Jake's death, sadness and gloom quickly spread over the town.

A cousin arrived to handle the funeral arrangements. They were simple and short, just the way Jake wanted. While his cousin was going through his belongings, he found boxes of love letters that had never been opened. They were returned and stamped "person unknown." Could it be this was all a charade? Was this lovely woman created by Jake? Did she ever exist, except in his mind?

His cousin was mystified because he heard Jake speak of his love so many times, and with such admiration and inner peace. As he shuffled through what seemed to be hundreds of love letters, he could not resist reading a few. There were phrases like, "I want to be your catalyst for peace of mind and your reinforcement for your inner well being." "You are wonderfully wonderful, and I consider myself to be a very blessed man, as I am enriched through knowing you."

Jake's cousin reached a compassionate decision. A small amount of his ashes and a few of the love letters would become a part of Jake's memorial service, for the town. Five love letters were selected from the five-year span of these letters. They were placed in five jars, along with a portion of his ashes, and sealed.

Then Jake's cousin and many of the town folks walked slowly down to the harbor carrying lighted candles. No words were spoken, just eyes focused out to the sea, with thoughts and many questions about

Jake hanging heavily in the air. The bottles with ashes and love letters were tossed in the sea, along with hundreds of roses.

On this warm evening night, a full moon shines over rapidly moving sea waters. The bottles bobbing up and down, then floating out farther and farther until they can no longer be seen. Jake's traveling heart perhaps will reach a lovely lady who will appreciate receiving a love letter.

VILLAREMI: A FAMILY MEMOIR
Lucy Rau Ferguson

On a spring day in 1886, Remi Chabot had come to inspect a property in the Napa Valley, available by forced sale for nonpayment of taxes. The 180 acres nestled between hills four miles northeast of Saint Helena. Part of the land, flat, arable and neglected, ran along one side of Bell Creek. The rest stretched up to heavily wooded hillsides – madrones, scrub oaks, Manzanita, the spikes of evergreens defining the skyline. Driving the unpaved county road in his hired buggy, Remi noted that about sixty acres climbed a steep hillside acoss the creek. Here he discovered a set of springs that would supply abundant water, even through the parched summers. Returning to a primitive wooden bridge that spanned the creek at the other end of the property, he took a narrow dirt lane that led up to the house.

Rem hitched the placid horse to a convenient post and knocked briskly at the front door of a square redwood farmhouse badly in need of fresh paint. He had been told that the owner, an alcoholic preacher who had fallen deeply in debt, would be home. Pounding with increasing vigor was to no avail. He was about to give up when he felt a tug on the dusty sleeve of his topcoat and looked down into a pair of very blue, not entirely guileless eyes. The tanned features framed by a pair of jug ears belonged to a skinny lad of about eight, barefoot and wearing the much laundered shirt and bib overalls of a farmer's child.

"He's in there but he won't hear you, not this time of day."

"I understand. What's your name?"

The boy had no difficulty with Remi's faint French Canadian accent. Pausing to inflate his narrow chest, "Artemus Leander Atwood. We live cross the crick. Most folk call me Artie. I can show you 'round if you like."

Remi, seeing little alternative, accepted the offer. It soon became clear that Artie was acquainted with every outbuilding, pool in the creek, tree and rock, and he must have roamed the ranch frequently. Preacher Todhunter sometimes hired him to do odd jobs. As they branched out from the immediate surroundings of the house, Remi was pleased to note, on south and west facing hillsides, the hillocks and struggling remains of grapevines. They had obviously succumbed to the phylloxera epidemic that had ravaged the vines a few decades ago. Remi knew that the vines could be replaced by French vinifera grapes grafted onto wild California rootstock that would resist the infestation. The underlying red clay soil was laced with fragments of obsidian from the neighboring extinct volcano. Artie proudly produced from a pocket several arrowheads he had found in a shallow cave the local Native Americans had used as a workshop.

"This is a good one. You kin keep it. I can always find more."

Remi thanked the boy, but he knew that his wife Emily, who had emigrated with her parents from Lyon as a small child, would be even more interested in the prospect of a productive vineyard in conditions that so closely mirrored the Rhone Valley of her childhood. Once the tour was over, Remi felt little need to rouse the owner from his alcoholic slumber. He could conclude the sale through agents in the Napa County land office. He handed Artie a five dollar gold piece, an enormous fortune to a poor farm child in the 1880's.

"Anytime in the future you want a job just come and let us know."

Once the family arrived from Oakland, Emily began to refurbish the old farmhouse and they settled in to "Villaremi" as their summer home. Artie and Kate, the third of the four Chabot daughters, discovered that they were exactly the same age. They shared many interests, especially in the animal life of the ranch, domestic and wild. After chores were done, they spent happy hours wading in the creek in search of pollywogs, salamanders, turtles, water snakes and occasional crawfish. These last they carefully collected in a bucket, using a pair of twigs as chopsticks to evade the fierce claws, and delivered them to the cook, Lem Yoey, at the kitchen door.

In adolescence their interests diverged. Artie took a variety of jobs, even as far away as Arizona working on the railroad. Meanwhile Kate did her best to conform to expectations for a proper Victorian young lady. She always stood out physically among her sisters. By fifteen she had reached her adult height of six feet, and towered over them, especially Clara, the youngest. Eventually the gangly adolescent grew into a handsome woman with erect carriage. When I, her only grandchild, came to know her in her fifties, her fighting weight was 180 pounds, but she was never obese, just impressive. Her temperament fluctuated between flashes of violent temper and great gentleness, especially to sick animals or children, anyone truly unfortunate. When I was a small child the anger frightened me, but I came to recognize that the outbursts were triggered when she felt disrespected or out of control in some way. At thirty she was left a widow with two very small daughters, a circumstance that contributed to an underlying sadness I also came to understand.

The three younger Chabot sisters inherited Villaremi at Emily's death in 1916. (Henrietta, the oldest was living on a farm near Santa Cruz with her husband and children.) Artie had returned, and true to Remi's promise they had hired him as full-time "foreman," living with his wife in a smaller house on the property. Artie was an indifferent farmer but a talented jack of all trades. He especially enjoyed any jobs, like clearing trails,that took him out into the woods. He had the keen senses of a born woodsman. He attributed his knowledge of the ways of the wild creatures to his Indian grandmother. He served as patient caretaker for three generations of Chabot children, including me, always letting us ride the farm horses to pasture, have a turn at driving the hay wagon, and trail along through the woods, as long as we observed safety rules, especially with guns. He taught us to become expert shots but never to kill wantonly for sport and was quietly scornful of those who never learned to tread softly.

By mutual agreement, the sisters left Artie's supervision mainly to Kate. Their discussions resembled the well-practiced arguments of an old married couple more than those of employer and employee, perhaps a carryover from their childhood relationship. Sometimes Kate lost patience, and the resulting shouts in her operatic mezzo soprano could be heard from one end of the 180 acres to the other. With increasing age, Artie claimed to be a bit hard of hearing. When he and his wife Lottie finally retired to a small cottage on the other side of the creek, much of the spirit of Villaremi went with them.

KATE'S WINE
Lucy Rau Ferguson

I am not sure just how or when Kate became the winemaker of the family. Presumably she fell heir to this role because there was no male to take it on. The two boys Emily bore died shortly after birth. Remi and Emily had planned a commercial winery and hired Italian stonemasons to construct a beautiful and efficient two-story cellar, built into the hillside in such a way that a large vaulted door opened on each level. It stands to this day, its date of 1888 carved into the stone, showing only a few tiny cracks from occasional earthquakes. The twenty-five acres of vineyard required no irrigation once the vines were well started. Predating the modern fashion for strict varietals, the red wine grapes planted on the flat acres were a mixture of mainly cabernet and pinot noir. The rows of white grapes, sauvignon blanc, golden chassler, and some other varieties no longer popular, were terraced up the south-facing hillside. They ripened earlier than any others in the valley. The grape terraces were punctuated halfway up by a row of olive and chestnut trees. They were planted so close together that a tractor could not possibly have driven between them without uprooting the vines. Many years of slow cultivation with horse and plow sculpted terraces like the ones on the hillsides of Tuscany or the steep slopes along the Rhone. My mother always maintained she could taste the flintiness in the wine from the volcanic soil.

As the vineyard first came into production a French winemaker was hired. Fifty years later we found remnants of his early experiments, including some bottles of angelica with beautifully engraved "Villaremi" labels, buried in a small storage cellar under the foreman's house. After Remi's death in 1890, Emily seems to have given up the project of a commercial winery. It would not have been feasible anyway during the Prohibition years. There was no thought, however, of abandoning the vineyard, and Villaremi continued to function legally as a family winery until 1942.

As far back as my memory extends into the 1930's, Kate's role as the family winemaker was well established, probably predating Emily's death in 1916. Artie's work in the winery was subject to certain moral strictures; as a Seventh Day Adventist he never tasted the wine. Kate trained him to carry out the many tasks that required physical strength and periodic attention when the family was not in residence. He scalded and sulphured the oak barrels before they were filled with wine for aging and later packed the bottles in wooden boxes for distribution to the family households in Oakland. Artie carried out these chores with a kind of rueful humor that seemed to date back to their collaboration in childhood mischief.

By the time I was ten, the only child in my generation, I was apprenticed as the third member of the winemaking team and assigned tasks I could handle easily. A favorite was starting the flow of wine in the slim hose from the barrel at bottling time. This involved getting down on hands and knees on the floor of the cellar, head as low as possible, and sucking with all my might, taking care not to choke on the sudden flow of wine or spill too much of it before it reached the neck of the first bottle. The red wine left bright ruby puddles on the cement and permanent stains on my shirts and jeans. I enjoyed the bottle washing; we usually did it in the hottest part of the summer, a great way to keep cool. We recycled our bottles from year to year, darker glass for the red wine and lighter for the white, using old hundred-gallon barrels cut in half as wash tubs. Artie soaked the bottless in a scalding solution of washing soda in the first tub, and we swirled pellets of lead shot to scour out any residue resistant to the bottle brush. Then two rinses in cold water, and we set the bottles neck down in compartmented wooden boxes to drain. I became expert at the twist of the wrist that flushed out each bottle in a small whirlpool and happily ended each day soaked from chin to ankles.

Kate made wine the way she cooked. I never saw her consult a recipe, but she consistently produced magnificent French bourgeois cuisine, part of the family heritage from Lyon. Though she could be impulsive and even explosive at times, and Sunday evening family suppers never passed without a vociferous argument, Kate was infinitely patient with the wine. She nursed each barrel to maturity through several years of rackings and tastings. We rarely drank any vintage, especially the reds, at less than five years. She carried it all in her head and her refined palate, a process timed to the rhythm of the seasons and the tasks each brought. In the very rare years when a batch went bad, we teased her that a rat must somehow have drowned in that barrel, but no one ever seriously challenged her expertise. The only instrument she used was a hygrometer, to test the specific gravity and thus the sugar content of the juice, when the grapes seemed ripe to her. Once she and the instrument arrived at an understanding, the picking began with the white grapes.

The pickers were recruited from among the college students and other young people in the area, and might include any family members who were available. Using short knives with very sharp curved blades, they worked along the rows of vines dropping the bunches of grapes into wooden lug boxes. As these filled they were loaded onto a cart pulled by a patient, reliable old horse. The loaded cart was driven for the crush to the upper level of the wine cellar, where the press was set up on level ground outside the high vaulted door. The press combined features of biblical design with a bit of Kate's invention. Her nephew Philip, the family engineer, connected the press to electric power from the PG&E line across the creek. Stomping feet were replaced by a sort of hopper with parallel rotating cork rollers, into which the men dumped the boxes of grapes. The crushed grapes dropped into a circular basket composed of narrow vertical oak staves with gaps between them and a giant screw mechanism in the middle. This sat on an oak platform with shallow sides and a spout fitted into one of them. From the spout the white juice, actually greenish gold in color and so sweet it attracted clouds of bees, was collected and poured into huge fermenting barrels.

The process for red wine, once the later ripening bluish purple grapes developed sufficient sugar, was somewhat different. The crushed bunches of grapes were fed directly into wide oak vats. As the roiling fermentation worked the initial magic of microscopic yeasts turning grape sugar into alcohol, the stems were carefully raked out to avoid excessive tannin in the wine. After two or more weeks of initial fermentation, depending on the warmth of the early October days, the crushed grapes were returned to the press, weighted with heavy boards and screwed down. The juice was siphoned to another set of barrels for further fermentation, and the pumice returned to the orchard and vineyard as fertilizing mulch.

The vintage must have been carried out more or less in this fashion for a half century. The yield varied each year, but amounted to several hundred gallons immediately after the crush. Over the next three years the volume was reduced to about half through evaporation and successive rackings to dispose of the accumulated lees deposited in the bottom of the barrel. Sometimes the initial transfer from oak to glass was into five-gallon wicker jacketed demijohns, filled and tightly corked. This essentially stopped the fermentation process but allowed the wines, especially the reds, to age further before the final bottling into the usual "fifths." A third of the final number of bottles from each vintage was distributed to each sister's household in Oakland. As long as Kate and her two daughters continued to live in the "big house" on the corner of Perry and Chetwood streets, even after Emily's death, those two shares were combined. I imagine that household easily consumed its two-thirds share, since all family festive gatherings, regular Sunday suppers, holidays and dinner parties, took place there.

When her older daughter Catherine had marred and was living in Paris, Kate finally decided to build her own house on the lot on MacArthur (then Perry Street) that Emily had apportioned to her. The lot ran very deep and Kate had gradually landscaped it with camellias, rhododendrons and other flowering shrubs and trees that provided a jungle-like barrier against the sound of increasingly busy traffic. At the back of the property she built the closest approximation to a small Tuscan villa she and the architect could devise. She furnished it lavishly with carved walnut and mahogany furniture and oriental carpets. She and Alice, her younger daughter, moved in just ahead of the stock market crash in 1929.

Among other amenities, one end of the deep basement was fitted out as a wine cellar. The location ensured a temperature that never varied much from sixty degrees. Wooden shelves lined the walls, notched to hold bottles, with unopened cases stacked at lower levels. Kate stored the cases of each subsequent vintage and a few going back to earlier years. She presided over her last vintage in the fall of 1942. By that time the country was deeply engaged in World War II. All the young men we depended on as pickers were enlisting or conscripted. Even Philip, then in his thirties but unmarried, was drafted early the following year. We brought in that last vintage mostly by our own labor as a family. Even I was allowed to skip the first couple of weeks of school and picked with a will. The hillside rows of vines were so deeply terraced I could reach the bunches of grapes without stooping and keep up with the other pickers. The filled lug boxes were too heavy for me to lift, but Artie would come to my assistance and heave them into the old wooden cart. I loved every moment of those days and remember them haloed in the warm golden light of late September. I have an enlarged copy of a snapshot Uncle Henry took, showing Artie and Philip pushing the long handle to crank the press, with Kate supervising. I always think of that photo as titled "The Last of the Wine." After that vintage the vines received no further care. I the late 1950's the vineyard was replanted entirely in cabernet sauvignon grapes and leased to Beringer.

Kate continued to nurture her wine until that final vintage was bottled three years later. By that time she was almost seventy and glad to be relieved of the physical labor. She was plagued by a chronic back condition and spent most mornings propped up in bed, carrying on a vigorous social life on the telephone.

Though her disposition had mellowed, she was still given to occasional rages, and we would warn her jokingly that she should calm down or she would have a stroke.

Our humor proved unfortunately prophetic. One Sunday in the late fall of 1955 she and my mother had just finished lunch when she keeled over in her chair. Once she was rushed to the hospital, the diagnosis of a massive cerebral hemorrhage was obvious. Much as we grieved for her, we were grateful that she lingered only for a couple of weeks. I cannot imagine how she would have tolerated living on, paralyzed and aphasic.

Kate's well-stocked wine cellar survived her. For a time, Catherine considered moving into her mother's house, even though the neighborhood was not what it had been. At that point the State of California as *deus ex* (or pro) *machina* intervened, condemning all the property on that side of MacArthur Boulevard in order to build the 580 freeway. The house was cleared, and my mother took her share of the proceeds to buy a fine house in the Berkeley hills. That came with an extended view of the Bay and the Golden Gate and a storage cellar in the basement. She salvaged the camellias and rhododendrons from Kate's garden and the contents of the wine cellar. We were still drinking Kate's wine a quarter century after her death, hoarding the last few bottles for special occasions. Some were "over the hill," but others were superb. We drank them reverently, toasting her memory.

AUNT KATY'S NEW HOBBY
Maimie Gimble

I shuffled impatiently at the station, awaiting the arrival of the train carrying Aunt Katy, my grandmother's niece. Finally, the train screeched to a halt. Under five feet tall, Aunt Katy was dressed gloomily, with her brown hair pulled severely into a bun. In one hand she carried a portmanteau, in the other, a plaid knitting bag with wooden handles. Most recognizable of all were her high-button shoes. The year was 1938. High-button shoes simply were no longer in fashion. It was as if Aunt Katy had been frozen in time since the day she received the news that her fiancé had been killed in France, only weeks before the signing of the Armistice pact bringing an end to World War 1.

I had never found her easy to talk with, always fearful my youthful enthusiasm may interrupt her gloom. I carried her knitting bag, a privilege allowed to few. The contents of Aunt Katy's knitting bag were an ongoing source of family amusement. Year after year, she travelled throughout London with a man's unfinished, navy sock on four steel knitting needles. Rumor had it that despite the constant clicking of her needles, the sock never grew in length and it was the same sock still in process. Aunt Katy revealed to me later that over the years she had knitted hundreds of pairs of socks for hospitalized soldiers.

Imagine my amazement, when, upon opening her knitting bag, she removed not the legendary sock, but a length of delicate dotted Swiss material, a spool of white thread and a fine sewing needle. "What about the socks?" I blurted out.

"I do not recall ever being told that I was permitted only to knit socks," she replied. "I'm smocking a dress for my landlady's new granddaughter."

"Why is so much fabric needed if it's for a baby?" I questioned, as Aunt Katy set out the wide piece of fabric. She explained that three times the width of the finished dress was required for smocking. I had seen smocking on infant dresses in expensive shops, but I never dreamed such beautiful, intricate work could result from the hands of mere mortals. I asked the purpose of the hundreds of tiny blue transfer dots ironed onto the wrong side of the material in evenly spaced rows. "That's enough questions for one day" she replied, almost smiling, "just watch."

Obediently, I watched in silence as she measured a length of cotton, slightly longer than the width of the fabric, knotted one end of the thread, and threaded the needle. She picked up the first dot, placing the threaded needle on the right side of the dot and taking it through the material towards herself on the left side of the dot, thereby creating a tiny stitch. Looking at the hundreds of dots, I could not imagine anyone having the patience to repeat this monotonous motion, but as she continued, I found myself hypnotized.

"Aunt Katy, would you please teach me to smock?" I heard myself say. "Why ever did I say that?" I wondered, without regret.

I looked up to see my parents exchange glances. Me, Aunt Katy, smocking? None of this made any sense, yet I knew it was exactly what I wanted, even if I didn't understand why.

"Smocking takes a lot of time, and infinite patience, but if you're certain you want to learn, I'll gladly teach you," she replied, as she looked into her bag and brought out a much smaller piece of material onto which the dots had been ironed - my practice piece. This unremarkable exchange was the beginning of an unusual friendship and a lifetime of delight, brought by the creation of so many beautiful handmade garments.

I was so grateful for that. Whatever her faults, Aunt Katy was blessed with unlimited patience. An undefined closeness developed between us as we sat together–sewing. I never regretted my impulsive quest to learn to smock. Aunt Katy continued to visit us, never without knitting or sewing projects. She had told me that once the basic smocking stitches had been learned, the only limitation was one's imagination. She taught me patience and perseverance.

"Anything worth doing is worth doing well" was another of her oft-repeated platitudes. Compliments from her were few and far between, but when given were so precious. She once commented that my smocking was really quite good, and she hoped one day I would know the joy of daughters for whom I could smock. Was she bequeathing me her own unfulfilled dream? Aunt Katy never lived to know I was blessed with three daughters, five grand-daughters, and eleven great-grandchildren, eight of whom are girls, but I somehow believe she knows.

THE BROWN CHAIR
Joyce Gubelman

It was huge, or so it seemed, in our apartment's small living room. I bought it at a Macy's warehouse sale shortly after moving to San Francisco in 1973. It was fake leather, "Naugahyde," I think it was labeled. Aesthetically it was pretty ugly, but it was so-o-o comfortable; not only did it rock back and forth, but it swiveled. The chair was cool in the summer and, adding a woolen blanket, cozy in the winter. In the evenings, my seven-year-old daughter and I would sit together in our big brown chair as I read to her, or we would watch TV, cuddle, or talk about our day.

During the next several years, my daughter often sat in the brown chair while she did her homework; sometimes she would lie upside down and swing her legs over the back of the chair while chattering on the phone to her school friends. When we had company, we always steered our guest, whether girlfriend, boyfriend, relative, or neighbor, to the comfortable brown chair.

I hauled the chair around during three moves, from one apartment to another. Finally, in 1984, after my daughter had gone off to college and I was planning yet another move this time to southern California, I included the brown chair in a major garage sale. I sold my sewing machine, ironing board, household items, books and LPs, a few toys and stuffed animals even my daughter's beautiful half-size violin (the violin went to an elderly Russian immigrant music teacher who had been searching for a violin for his grandson). Throughout the day, I had several offers on the brown chair, but for some reason I hesitated.

Around four in the afternoon, I was about to "pack it in" when a very pregnant woman arrived, looked at the chair, and declared it PERFECT! She told me she wanted to sit in a big comfortable chair instead of a wooden rocker, to nurse her soon-to-be-born baby. We immediately arrived at a price and she arranged for her husband to pick it up the next day. That night I went to bed exhausted, but happy, knowing that the big brown chair would be going to a good home.

SOME FISH!
Joyce Gubelman

There were record snowfalls in the Sierras that year. People were still skiing on the Fourth of July and Tioga Pass into Yosemite remained closed. Children were out of school for the summer and my sister Lulu had arranged to sublet a friend's condo in Mammoth Lakes for a few days. We packed up her big yellow van, piled in with the kids (my daughter Erin, and Lulu's Laura and Andrew), and drove to Mammoth in the eastern Sierras. After a long drive, we found the condo, settled in, and went to bed early. The next morning we rented inner tubes and, shrieking with glee, we slid down a huge snow-covered hillside. An official looking man in a snowplow appeared on the scene and we thought he was going to chase us away, but instead he cheerfully carved out a mini-ski run just for us. We slid, full-speed, down the hill on our inner tubes most of the day until we were all too exhausted to trudge up to the top one more time.

The following day, we drove to Mono Lake where we walked around and marveled at the weird tufa formations and the many birds around the lake, then drove to Lee Vining, a town about 25 miles from Mammoth. From Lee Vining we drove north along miles and miles of dirt road to Bodie State Park where we explored the gold-mining ghost town there. Only a small percentage of the buildings remain of this once wild gold-mining town of over 10,000 people, mostly "badmen," in its 1880 heyday. The streets and remaining wooden structures are eerily quiet now, as quiet as "Boot Hill" just outside of the three fenced-in cemeteries located at the edge of the town.

Back at Mammoth the next day, the snows were melting, wildflowers were blooming, waterfalls were plunging down the mountainsides, and the rivers and streams were rushing. Someone suggested we go fishing, so we found a local bait shop where we bought fishing licenses and rented fishing gear. We settled in on a rocky outcrop overlooking a rapidly flowing stream, baited our hooks with cheese balls or "red balls of fire" salmon eggs (in Laura's words, "not as gross as worms"), and cast our lines into the water. Andrew, our youngest, threw his line behind him, and flipped it up and out towards the stream, but before it hit the water, the hook snagged on a tree above him. Andrew's response was "How the heck did that happen?" Throughout the day, "How the heck did that happen?" became our stock phrase for whenever a line got snarled or didn't go where we expected it to. Erin and I were content to put our lines in the water and watch the cliff swallows darting about, building their nests across the river from where we sat. Meanwhile Andrew, who knew no fear, ventured farther and farther out on the rocks and Lulu was worried that he would lose his footing and fall into the fast-running, ice-cold river, so we packed up our gear and moved on to fish the lakes in the June Lake Loop. We didn't have many bites, but no one seemed to mind; the day was achingly beautiful, as if the world had just been created anew. I was happy to be breathing in the fresh mountain air, gazing at the snow-clad peaks and the wildflowers blanketing the hillsides, and lazily casting my line again and again into the water. Towards the end of the day, we heard Laura give a yelp, then yell for her mom to "get the net, get the net!" She then reeled in a good-sized trout which Lulu, with Andrew's help, managed to get into the net. When we got back to the bait shop to return our gear, we learned that Laura's fish was the largest fish caught so far that year. She agreed to having it packed on ice and showcased in the window for a day.

Today, a grown-up Laura is a teensy bit blasé about the size of the trout, saying that she caught bigger fish in Lake Michigan when she stayed with her grandparents in Wisconsin. But I remember how proud she was that day, when many of the local fishermen at June Lake admired her trout and asked her where exactly she had caught it and what kind of bait she used.

On our last evening at Mammoth Lakes, we pan-fried Laura's trout in lemon and butter over a campfire and, as we all agreed, it was mighty delicious!

SANONG AND ME
Joyce Gubelman

I was between jobs, and because of corporate restructuring, my previous position, which I had loved, had been eliminated. I was feeling down in the dumps as I updated my resume and began searching for a new job. My friend Harriet, a therapist, suggested that in the interim I should do some volunteer work as a way to focus on others, rather than just myself. It was good advice.

I love the English language and had been an English major in college, so I decided that a reading or literacy project might be a good fit. I found an English as a Second Language (ESL) Program at the YMCA in San Francisco's Tenderloin District that needed volunteers. The Refugee Women's Program (RWP) was a part of the Refugee Community Program sponsored by the Northern California Ecumenical Council. RWP's clients initially were women refugees from Southeast Asia, Latin America, Eastern Europe and Ethiopia, but the organization evolved to also include men and families from those countries. I made a time commitment and underwent several weeks of ESL training at RWP. I learned how to teach the basics of finding one's way around a neighborhood, shopping, using money, going to the bank and the post office, and riding public transit. I made flashcards with pictures of clothing – shirts, blouses, skirts, trousers, shoes and socks, as well as pictures of fruits, vegetables, firetrucks, policemen, buses, taxicabs, etc. I practiced role-playing exercises using gestures, body language, and facial expressions. I learned to make color rods to teach the names of colors and to create a family tree to teach words for family relationships.

Finally, the day arrived when training had been formally completed and we volunteers were to be assigned a family or an individual to teach. Roun, the staff member for outreach to Cambodian and East African families, told me my placement was to work with a Hmong from Cambodia; I was confused because I thought the Hmong people were from Laos. It turned out that Roun was saying (he had a slight accent) "a monk from Cambodia." There seemed to be a bit of serendipity at play here in my assignment because I had recently been exploring Buddhism and learning to meditate. However, I immediately felt totally inept at the thought of teaching English to a Buddhist monk; most of my training at RWP now appeared to be almost useless, since teaching English around the basics of going to the bank, the grocery store, or the post office did not apply. A monk does not do any of those things, nor does he go shopping, nor wear western clothing. My imagination was challenged in finding lesson material relevant to his experience and interests, so I spent hours at the public library poring over the the Project Read section, scouring bookstores for ideas in lesson planning, and utilizing RWP resources.

Roun took me for my initial visit to the Nagara Dhamma Temple located in the Outer Sunset District where I was introduced to the Venerable Phra Sanong Taveekoon who was born in Cambodia, but lived most of his life in Thailand. Roun had explained to me that many monks now serving the Cambodian community are from Thailand because so many Cambodian monks died during the horrific "killing fields" under the Khmer Rouge regime during the 1970's and that Theravada Buddhism is the form of Buddhism practiced in both Cambodia and Thailand. The Venerable Sanong Taveekoon was currently the senior monk at this Cambodian temple. He asked me to call him Sanong, his given name. He told me he had studied English in Thailand, but discovered on his flight to San Francisco that he couldn't understand a word the airline pilot or the flight attendants were saying; he had learned English from a Thai with that teacher's Thai pronunciation. Thus, I became a tutor/mentor, rather than a teacher, as we focused on pronunciation, sentence structure, and English slang. I found that I didn't have to develop rigid lesson plans, but rather, let each weekly session guide the next one. If a subject piqued his interest, I found material on it for the next week and built an English lesson around that topic. He had a keen mind and was interested in many subjects, and he also possessed a delightful sense of humor. He often watched CNN news and would have questions for me as to national and world events and what they meant. Sometimes, he had a computer question – I marveled that he was computer literate and that the temple computer was programmed to print in Cambodian, Thai, and English. Sometimes, a temple board member or another monk would sit in on our ESL sessions and we would have lively discussions. Once, the temple van wouldn't start, so I manned the steering wheel while the saffron-robed monks pushed to get it started. One Saturday afternoon, Sanong and a junior monk took public transportation and came to my apartment in Noe Valley for tea. My daughter was home from college that weekend and thought the monks were "really cool."

Meanwhile, I had started a new job. Sometimes I was exhausted after a long day at work and wished I could go directly home, put my feet up, and relax with a glass of wine instead of going on to the temple. When I got there, though, I felt rejuvenated; the temple was a little oasis of peace and tranquility. I would arrive, often bringing flowers for the altar, ring the doorbell, put my hands together and bow slightly as I was ushered inside. I slipped off my shoes and took my place on a cushion, surrounded by images of the Buddha and the fragrance of incense, far away from the noise of the outside world. The elderly nun-in-residence would bring tea for us and set a plate of fruit or cookies in front of me; Sanong would chuckle and say, "Snack for you" (he thought "snack" a very funny word). I learned that monks eat nothing after the noon meal, ingesting only water, tea or juices until their next morning meal. Sanong taught me to say "Sawadeekha," a Thai greeting. He taught me the variations of "wei," the putting together of one's hands and bowing which is a gesture of respect or a "hello without words" in Thailand. I learned about the cultures of Cambodia and Thailand and I developed a greater empathy for refugee life in America. Not only did I relearn aspects of my own English language, but I learned a few words of Thai, and I learned more about Buddhism; kindness and compassion ceased to be mere words to me as I saw these qualities personified in Sanong. I learned so much more than I taught, and my life was enriched by my time with Sanong. Two years later he went back to Thailand, but phoned me when he returned for a brief visit several years ago. I still miss him and he will always have a special place in my heart.

TCHOTCHKES
Ruth Guthartz

Tchotchkes The Yiddish word tastes as sweet and smooth as my mother's tea laced with honey. I hear her low, warm voice telling me that the bric-a-brac atop my tall living room bookcase are only *tchotchkes*: knickknacks, trifles. I stand there, ready to dust them as she goes on, "They aren't worth anything," Mama would have said. "They're not valuable."

"Not so," I tell her, or wish I could, to bridge the miles across this month's anniversary of her death almost sixty years ago.

The tchotchkes have no theme. There's no apparent link among them. They seem to fulfill a definition in Rosten's *The Joy of Yiddish* : "an accumulation of miscellaneous or unimportant stuff." They're not like the old Horatio Alger books my husband Jack found in the used bookstores he haunted. He bought and collected those books as though they were treasures.

The fact is that Mama's assessment would have a degree of accuracy. There are a few trifles up there, like the little brown ceramic stub-tailed deer, a gift from a never-to-be- forgotten friend. Hella was the closest friend, almost a sister, I ever had. Together we celebrated our birthdays, five days and five years apart, for more than twenty years, until Alzheimer's claimed her.

The smallest trifle is an ivory carving, a *netsuke*, that Herb, Jack's kid brother, sent from Japan in 1945, when he was in the Army. Three thousand miles apart, once a year, Herby and I phone New Year greetings and exchange tales of our grandchildren.

My *tchotchkes* have stories buried behind their facades that few people, not even I, know.

Who can tell why an unknown artist carved – from a piece of dark oak, then smoothed and polished that wood till it gleamed – a bird that resembles a crane. The tall, slender, sinuous body lacked wings, but I saw it long ago as a bird whose head looked skyward, whose bill seemed to be making an important announcement before taking flight. Its claws clasped a piece of rough, unpolished driftwood in which were embedded three mysterious large nails at the base; they might have guarded the fowl. When I first saw that creature in a shop window at Stinson Beach, where Jack, the kids and I vacationed for several summers, I fell in love with it. But the tag revealed a price too expensive for my limited pocketbook, so I put the thought out of my mind. Still, I never really forgot that bird. And I've never forgotten Stinson Beach.

It's really Seadrift, where most of the modest houses are rented by the week or month, when the owners are traveling. We rented either the Leonard house on the ocean front, or the Welcome house on the lagoon side. Neither had a TV, which I considered a blessing, but both were stocked with playing cards and many board games.

Seadrift was a time and place to get back to myself: to reading, listening to music, knitting and cross-stitching and just wool-gathering. At night the murmuring ocean waves put me to sleep; the morning and evening fog settled over the highway like a blanket that protected me from the outside world. My kids, though, greeted it in the mornings with groans of dismay.

A trip into town to stop at the library, to shop for groceries or to window-shop in the few small stores satisfied my urge for activity. It was on one of these trips to town that I saw the bird, loved it and banished it from memory.

Until months later, on Valentine's Day? An anniversary? One of the times when Jack and I traditionally exchanged gifts, I unwrapped and opened a large box.

There was the bird.

I patted the smooth head, caressed the long, alluring curves down to the driftwood on which the creature rested. Without hesitation I named it "Adlai"; every creature has to have a name, doesn't it? That was in honor of the gentleman who was, perhaps, too dignified a person to be our president.

There is something Mama might consider valuable, a memento from the sabbatical Jack and I took in 1973—a prayer book, a *siddur*, about the size of an inch-thick stack of 3x5 index cards. Its silver cover is embellished with two Stars of David and a turquoise stone in each corner. A border of Hebrew letters translates, "How goodly are your tents, O Jacob." The flyleaf inscription reads, "Nov. 1973. To Ruth, as a remembrance of our trip to Ha-eretz, Jack."

When I read these words aloud now, so many years later, they have a bittersweet taste. I wish I'd kept a journal of that month because I remember so little of that time, even though, as the family historian, people have always turned to me to ask about dates and places. Even Jack complained, more than once, that I usually remembered too much.

I anticipated that trip in 1973 with many misgivings about the differences Jack and I were often experiencing; the heightened concern about the sudden, dreadful Yom Kippur war in Israel added to my indecision. I see-sawed for days about leaving. But Jack wanted more than ever to help the Israelis celebrate their victory, while I shrank from what felt like a condolence call for the loss of lives in that six-day war.

We stayed in Jerusalem at the YMCA (called the Yimcha) across the street from the elegant King David Hotel. Our small room held a closet, a chest of drawers, a night table and twin beds. We could have talked, reached over, held hands to close that small space between our beds, but we didn't. Communication, never our strong point, remained on a chit-chat level. How could we resolve conflicts we hadn't acknowledged, no less named? Pleasant in a distant sort of way, we were no more than slightly affectionate.

Despite that, as I look back, I wonder if that was when we learned we shared more similarities than differences. Maybe in Israel, among the blackout curtains and unreadable Hebrew street signs, we felt our fragility and knew what we didn't want to throw away.

So, standing in front of the tall bookcase with all the *tchotchkes*, I'm relieved to turn to the trifle in the middle of the display, a little handmade accordion book, its cover a light-grey marbled paper with streaks of blue and darker grey.

I look back with fondness for the years I spent learning calligraphy and to this book that testifies to my achievement. The first page displays a bluebird in flight, the other pages are imprinted with a black-ink, hand-calligraphed quotation, except for two red-inked words: WHY AND HOW. The quotation, an excerpt from an essay by the dramatist Lorraine Hansbury reads:

> *The WHY of why we're here is an intrigue for adolescents; the HOW is what must command the living. Man is unique in the universe, the only creature who has in fact the power to transform the universe. Therefore, it does not seem unthinkable to me that man might just do what the apes never will—impose the reason for life on life itself. I wish to live because life has within it that which is good, that which is beautiful and that which is love. Therefore, since I have known all these things, I have found them to be reason enough and . . . I wish to live. Moreover, because this is so, I wish others to live for generations and generations and generations.*

I wrote that in calligraphy three years after Jack's death, two years after my two oldest grandchildren were born. I wished Jack had been there to share our being grandparents, to tell those girls the same silly bedtime stories he'd told our children.

I dust Adlai and the *siddur*; I move an infinite bit of space between the *tchotchkes* in the bookcase, and I tell myself that Mama was right. They aren't worth anything; they're not valuable. Truth is, they're absolutely priceless.

CHICKEN CHECKMATE
Betsy Hess-Behrens

There were two main problems with our family in the early thirties: first, we were very sentimental, especially about holidays; and second, we were very poor for a while. You see, Dad was a high school teacher when the big depression hit and the city had no money to pay teacher salaries except in script. So there were many economy measures that often proved an adventure to my brother, sister, and me but must have been difficult for our folks at times.

Holidays were particularly trying for them. Everything had to be handmade from saved odds and ends that showed promise of having potential in the silk purse/sow's ear department. This took a lot of time, imagination, and spirit--which was often hard to come by when things were so very bleak. However, the gifts, celebrations and vacations from those years are among our most treasured memories (and perhaps the subject for another article later).

Easter presented a special problem however. Easter dresses and a new shirt for my brother could be sewn from leftover remnants, but how could Mom and Dad find a substitute for the Grand Easter Basket and Egg Hunt that they knew we would be expecting? It was, after all, pretty hard to make jelly beans, gorgeous big chocolate bunnies, and cream-filled chocolate eggs decorated with candy rosettes out of anything recyclable in the house. But, as usual, they came up with a solution that made us feel the most envied kids on the block, rather than the most deprived.

They bought six newly hatched baby chicks from the nearby farmer. In those days, the nearby farmer lived just outside the city limits, not miles past endless suburbs and shopping malls. This was the bargain: our family would take care of the chicks until they were past the fragile stage. We children would have the fun of watching the tiny Easter chicks tumble around and grow strong enough to be petted, and then, a few weeks after the holidays, Dad would sell them back to the farmer for a small profit.

There was just one small hitch in their plan, which did not become evident until long after the excitement of Easter morning had passed. And what a special morning that was! We were told that instead of hunting throughout the house for several baskets apiece, we should look for one big nest to share that was hidden in the kitchen. Our curiosity overcame any disappointment we might have felt and we scurried to the kitchen as fast as our little legs would take us. We didn't have to look long; we heard them before we saw them--tiny little peeps coming from a big box underneath the kitchen stove (you could clean and put things under stoves in those days.) We could hardly wait to peek in. There they were: six butter-colored little puff balls of life huddled together under the warmth of the light bulb Dad had rigged up in our homemade incubator. They were still too young to move about much, so they mostly just peeped and flopped around a bit, usually on top of one another. We were not allowed to touch them until they became stronger, but we took great delight in watching that process take place right under our own eyes and in our very own kitchen. Of course, we became sort of neighborhood celebrities and there was a steady stream of visitors in and out of our private "Nature Center." Mom and Dad hadn't counted on that. Nor had they counted on the rapidity with which the chicks would become chickens.

Much too soon they outgrew the confines of their makeshift incubator, so Dad solved their temporary housing needs by enclosing the four stove legs with a length of chicken wire he had scrounged from somewhere and adding layers of gravel, newspaper, and cardboard on the floor to complete their substitute shelter. It was time for a family conference about the fate of the chickens who by now all had pet names.

One of them was Chicken Little and another was Henny Penny, I believe, but the other names have all been filed away under the heading of "Memory Loss."

This conference was a solemn occasion. We children could tell right away because Dad poured homemade root beer for each of us, and ale (also a product of our basement brewery) for himself and Mom. It was a cozy scene: we all sat around our enamel-topped kitchen table, a wall lamp over the sink gave a warm glow to the gathering, and the chickens provided background music with a medley of contented cluckings, scratchings, and occasional feeble attempts at crowing sounds.

"Now, children, ahem, these chickens have been fun for us and very educational too, but they need more room and of course your mother would like to have her kitchen back as a nice, clean, quiet kitchen instead of a chicken coop. Also, they didn't eat much as baby chicks, but now it's becoming too much trouble and expense to keep them fed. So the time has come for us to sell them back to the farmer. We'll make a nice outing of it this Sunday and you can all write compositions about the experience for your teachers."

Somehow the opportunity to write an essay didn't seem much of a reward. Nor did our mother's offer to help us illustrate our stories. Actually we didn't even consider it at all, but immediately set up such a howl that we frightened the chickens who, in turn, set up their own hullabaloo with such raucous squawking that Mom and Dad turned up the radio real loud in the hopes of drowning out the noise so the neighbors wouldn't hear. Over this cacophony of sound, Mom and Dad both tried to be heard and thus added to the earsplitting din. I would like to add that Chicken Little ran around shouting, "The sky is falling!" but you wouldn't believe that part of my story.

Eventually it all calmed down, facilitated I suspect by the extra glasses of ale that helped our parents cope with our intransigence--for the moment at least. We sniffled our self-righteous sniffles and went to bed, convinced that we had won out over the grown ups this time. It wasn't long, however, before the next fowl furor arose to up-end the delicate balance of power between the worlds of child and adult.

It was on a lovely spring morning when we went to the kitchen for breakfast as usual, only to find that it was all most unusual. It seems that the chickens' overnight struggle for Lebensraum had resulted in a cave-in of their fragile wire enclosure and there were chickens, chickens everywhere, scratching, fluttering, and roosting all over the room.

"That's it! The chickens must go!" roared Dad. We could tell this was serious.

"But Daddy, what will happen to them?" We knew what would happen to them: in those days one did not buy a neat plastic-wrapped package of chicken parts all ready to be assembled into one whole chicken (as in a recent cartoon). Instead it was brought home with all its feathers still on and with its beady little eyes bugging out and its limp head and feet dangling from a very dead body. We three began to cry most piteously, and all at once.

"But, Daddy, you gave them to us. They are our pets! You can't kill our pets. Mama, don't let him take them back to the farmer, Mama, please!" Oh, we were good at this and getting better every moment: Divide and conquer!

That night it was settled—the great compromise. Keeping chickens outside in the yard was against the law (besides, what would the neighbors think), so we vacated the kitchen except for necessities and the daily cleaning, and temporarily "ate out" in the dining room (usually reserved for entertaining and the Sunday dinner). The chickens thus took over and ruled the roost, so to speak. But, the very next weekend we packed them all up in a makeshift coop which Daddy put in place of the removable trunk at the back of the car and the whole family (plus six noisy chickens) tried to sneak out of town at daybreak so the neighbors wouldn't see us. Daddy was very proud of his elegant, second-hand, green Oakland landau sedan (that he claimed had once belonged to a mid-Eastern prince) and was very embarrassed by the temporary alteration in style. But the trip was necessary to complete the other half of the bargain. It took all day to drive the 120 miles to our great-grandfather's farm near Lyons, New York, but when we got there we all breathed a sigh of relief. We children were happy because Great Grandpa banded our "pets" so that we could always identify them and insure their longevity; Great Grandpa was happy about the addition to his hen yard, and Mom and Dad returned to normal.

For a while the first thing we children did upon subsequent visits to the farm was a "chicken-check." Gradually we came to trust that all was well and would stay that way, and finally I guess the novelty wore off and we just forgot all about it. So it is very likely that one of our chickens eventually became the main course in the "Most Memorable Meal" contest run by one of the women's magazines.

THE DIAMOND RING
Betsy Hess-Behrens

I once had a husband who wrote a very scholarly tome about family life; it was well received in academia. But when I think of my own childhood, I sometimes suspect that Shirley Jackson, in her book called *Life Among the Savages,* had a more accurate take on the dynamics of shared domestic space.

I guess our Depression-Era flat was big enough for a family of five; it's just that even the Elephant House at the Buffalo Zoo would not have been big enough to contain all the tensions that trampled the psychic space between my sister and me. Now don't get me wrong; she turned out to be a very lovely person. I like to think I'm OK too.

Maybe it was the small double bed siblings had to share in those days. Twin beds or separate rooms were for rich kids or movie stars or some other kind of foreigner. Things were further complicated by the fact that ours was tucked into an alcove under the eaves. Maybe, because I was older and stayed up later, I got the outside and she got the inside.

"Mama, she's breathing on my neck!"

"But there's no air next to the wall. She wants me to die!"

"Mama, she's jiggling her foot!"

"But my foot fell asleep before I did, Mama. Does she want it to fall off from lack of circulation?"

"Mama, she's got the cat in bed!"

"Mama!" (This in unison.)

Poor Mama, she sighed a lot.

Naturally, the complexities of the territorial imperative spread beyond the boundaries of the bed and out into the room: to one of us, our bedroom was a hidden treasure-trove sans map; to the other it was a garbage dump where things got lost.

Well, you get the idea. Our big brother was another source of rivalry. Of course we competed for his attention because we both thought he was more interesting than either of us. Actually—he was!

Then, too, we were not immune from the Favorite Child battle for our parents' attention, although we were both pretty sure of being loved in general. Now, there's the catch: we each wanted to be loved in particular.

One would think that maturity would put all these childish feelings to rest, but despite the fact that we lived on opposite coasts, the balance scale was in constant use even after becoming rusty with age. It was so silly because, clearly, we had both chosen the life we had, and wouldn't have exchanged it for all the tea in China. I should mention, however, that we were both coffee drinkers.

Poor Mama was always in the middle, trying to assure us that she admired us equally and thought that we had both contributed fabulous genes to posterity. Success as career women was not an important consideration at that time; the feminist movement had barely knocked on glass doors let alone gazed up at the ceiling. She was proud of both our efforts nonetheless.

She also tried to show equal affection when giving us gifts, so everything was carefully measured out. Of course we rarely had an opportunity to compare them because we lived so far from each other. Besides I think we both had an unspoken agreement to keep our gifts hidden as a gesture of sibling comity. But we both must have wondered about some of the jewelry that we had admired and that she no longer wore. One of these was a coral necklace I remembered proudly wearing to a high school dance. When I casually asked Mom about it she became very upset, claiming that I must have lost it if I couldn't remember what I had done with it. Had my years of motherhood really left me so unhinged? My guilt and loss made me miserable until my sister happened to mention that it had been given to her long ago. I am ashamed to admit that my former misery gave way to a very pernicious jealousy. I tortured myself with the idea that maybe Mom had really meant it to be mine. But perhaps it is normal to have a wee streak of the masochist to enjoy at times.

There was one piece of jewelry, however, that had a special mystique to it: Mother's diamond engagement ring. It was the family jewel—perfect, brilliant, valuable. It was also imbued with touching sentiment, enriched by World War I history.

Mom hadn't wanted to marry because her choice of a nursing career was open only to single women at that time. Much as she found Dad a charming, handsome fellow, she felt no urgency to restrict her ambitions by marriage. The war and his sudden army transfer to the Curtis Airplane plant on Long Island changed all that. Despite her reluctance, his impassioned letters begging her to join him finally broke down her reserve. However, in 1918, a good girl couldn't live alone in New York City and carry on with a gentleman caller. So, within a week of accepting his proposal, she found herself at Tiffany's where he bought the precious, perfect diamond ring just hours before he made an honest woman of her at The Little Church Around The Corner.

We children were all born just before the Crash when our father's construction business went into bankruptcy because of defaulted second mortgages. Of course we didn't understand much about the grownups' world of finances, but we did know that it must have been pretty serious because his partner blew his brains out–that's the way people said it– "blew his brains out." We looked at our father's head for a long time after that. In our child's world it was just all very dark and gloomy. In hushed voices we were told that the little table-radio was a Christmas present for the children because our parents didn't dare buy anything for themselves during the bankruptcy proceedings.

Even Mama's precious diamond was kept secret and hidden. It hung on a little cup-hook screwed into the backside of the china cabinet in the dining room. I remember how I would pull the cabinet away just an inch so I could reach behind and sneak a look at it now and then. It was bright and shining and beautiful in all the darkness of those days. We were forbidden to tell anyone about it, or about the homemade wine hidden behind our chalkboard in the basement playroom. I guess all that stuff was sort of illegal, and that made it pretty exciting too. How they assured our secrecy, I don't remember. Maybe they threatened to give us two teaspoons of cod liver oil each morning instead of just one.

When things got better and Mama started wearing the ring again on special occasions, it seemed like everything felt brighter because she was so proud of it and happy to bring it out from its hiding place. After we all grew up and moved away, however, the ring just became another childhood memory except when she visited and its magic reasserted itself. On one of these occasions Mom took me aside to talk to me about her will. "I know you'll understand, honey, but I'm going to leave the ring to your sister. She never had a diamond engagement ring because her husband was just a poor student. All she ever had was a Zircon."

I know I didn't bite my tongue, but I must have choked on the words I held back when I really wanted to scream: "Good God, Mama, I was married twice and never had any engagement ring—not even one from a Cracker Jack box!"

So my sister was promised the ring and I was given the opportunity to wallow in smug, martyred magnanimity for many years to come. I held my tongue even when Mom showed off the new setting made to replace the weakened old Tiffany prongs. "Yes, it looks lovely, Mama, just as pretty as the original setting and now you won't have to worry about losing it." What a good girl am I.

Now it's a funny thing: I don't care much for jewelry, especially rings, so it must have had more to do with "Mama likes you best!" or some other symbolic residue of childhood anxiety during those Depression years. Nonetheless when Mom died more than twenty years ago, we were very careful to put the ring into my sister's possession while I wasn't paying attention. Best that way.

And so the years have passed, we are both in our eighties, and it has all been long forgotten. If I ever gave it a thought, most likely I just hoped that she had enjoyed wearing the ring and acknowledged to myself that—because she had such long, slender fingers—it probably looked better on her than it would have on me anyhow. And I don't remember how it happened that in our recent phone conversation the ring was mentioned again after all this time.

"Oh, didn't you know," my sister casually remarked, "some time ago I had the ring appraised and we discovered that when Mom had the new setting made, the jeweler substituted a Zircon in place of her diamond."

CAPRI: A SLIDE SHOW — ITALY, 1935
Roy M. Kahn

We did not stay in Ana Capri that summer. It was unfit for tourists, but good enough for Hadrian to throw his enemies off the cliffs to the sharks at sea, and for peasants. We stayed at the Las Palma, the second-best hotel by the piazza and the manager got his leg broken (for accepting Jews?) and hobbled for six weeks that summer.

And Monsignor Di Ferraro, the only priest on Capri, paralyzed from the waist down, conducting mass seated – the only such dispensation in Christendom – who knew all the gossip and details of marriages (and non-marriages) on the entire island, and taught my mother Italian by sharing unholy secrets.

And the unblessed, though wafer thin, sister contessas renting books from their villa to stay alive. (The Bobsey Twins my summer saviors).

Umberto rowed ashore – the crown prince with his unguarded female entourage – and ordered that I, aged 9, barefoot and dressed only in wet swim trunks, play Chopin while they all ate off gold-rimmed plates above the Picocola Marina.

And, later, my brother, 15, marched into the carabinieri and read them The Manifesto in Italian (while giving the Communist a salute.) We were all arrested, but they couldn't hold us, because of the Umberto thing...

And planes flying overhead on their way to bomb Ethiopia where towns and natives "opened up like black roses," according to Mussolini; Hailie Selasie at the League of Nations.

Ezra Pound shouted *"A IO ZAGREUS!"* and, much later, *"io pound"* came the echo.

Benito Benito Benito
TUTTO E FINITO !
Addesso:

High-rises on Ana Capri (the sharks no longer afraid of being thrown to the sea); the priests walk about; the peasants are blond and speak English; the governor is socialist, Hailie Selassie was murdered in his bed; and Ezra is with Zagreus (or Mussolini).

All as it should be.

Beneditto,   Benito,   Bene.

ON DOING THE LAUNDRY
Roy Kahn

What shall they think of me
when I am dead?

That I kept a neat house?

Or
that, while doing laundry I
thought of poems,
separating out the new and old sadnesses,
feelings far from daylight,
(old photographs, tinted in brown
and off-green shades of fading memory):

cold water for bright colors, warm for white;
cleansed by unfeeling granules
poured from new boxes.

Back and forthing – love and duty – life
and life past, until,

heavy with experience and weighting the final rinse,
wondering:

Will they say of me that I loved and
tendered my love anew each week, so they always
found the faded colors neatly folded,
renewed, with past forgotten?

Love finds its path in many ways.
Pain washes deep, restoring the lost,
destroying the past, and tendering the
present.

A drudge among the colors? ---
a passionate past ?
restoring over and over again
their auburns, red, yellows, greens and blues – creating
love again from grayed, discarded fabrics.

RENTED
Roy Kahn

I. A Trip to Nostalgia

In a room in life's hotel
I came upon myself and We
(the other me's and Me) –
saw
an aged man upon a stick
where straight was lost
and strings attached.

We sought to flee
(the me's and Me)
to hide from Me
where all the past years went
and where my ancient soul
was spent upon mine devil's cloven foot
that bears me yet:

Frescoes of taste;
an icebox of woulds;
bottled regrets
undone by time,
by triumph of waste

II.

Strings flexed, it danced –
a lonely tune;

*"kept the words, but
Lost the meaning;
Kept the notes –
but lost the Music".*

The hotel billed.
We'd thought it free;
it never is.

With hopeless hope
and naught to be:
We are as we are ---

Death pays all debts.

(With humble nods to Dante, Donne and Yeats).

STALAG X — 1945
(ON SEEING DACHAU)
Roy Kahn

When :   In the roar of silent hearing
           "*Schweinhuind!*" said the whip

Then: knelt the upright standing;
           prayed the shuffling feet;
           and motionlessly danced
           the *Chassidim*.

(On seeing Dachau in 1945)

UNTITLED
Roy M. Kahn

Three shadows move in a darkened room;
glide and putter their separate ways
pulling shades aright, askew
(the contradictory tasks
everyday done
and undone anew).

The soundless sun has abandoned its cries
but lies
among the shades in a darkened room
(gliding and puttering their separate ways),
helpless to raise the Blind to see
His impenetrable anonymity.

IN PRAISE OF OLDER MEN
Jennifer D. King

What a sight
an 80-year-old James Dean
requisite black leather jacket
white tee shirt
a silver haired prince
without a helmet
perched atop a tricked out Harley
his back
permanently bent into
the biker position

Disgusted
with the expectations of others
who say
-do volunteer work
-usher at the church
-collect the coins from all 50 states

Instead
he revs the engine
checks the mirror
hurls himself into the flow of traffic
confident that he has excellent insurance coverage

A CURE
Jennifer D. King

I'm wondering
if scientists came up with a pill
would the sick ones take it?
Would a medium dose of voltage loosen
organisms that makes the sick ones act out?

Is there a patch to suppress
malignant, raging tongues?
could 500 mg of *thoro somethingorother*
be enough
to unclench a fist
in time?

Could a weekly injection or *dextra whoknowswhat*
make us feel safer about taking a walk at night?
does a black heart just need to be
transplanted?

Probably not.

Better to keep the well ones
in custody
safe hideouts
somewhere soothing
designed to shield
to protect.

Better that the battered
bruised-ribbed and broken-nosed
damaged psyche, wrecked life
the well ones
remain behind the tall fenced,
steel framed, double paned
security guarded, coded entry
retreats–hospitals–care centers
until a cure for the sick ones is found.

WE ARE LIKE CHILDREN
Jennifer D. King

We are like children
dressed in adult clothing
You stumbling about in too-large daddy shoes
Me tripping in my mommy heels
being grown-up—doing grown-up
feet and hearts--- not fitting

We are like rain storms in the desert
Your dark thunderclouds
threatening to break over us
My parched earth waiting, wanting to be watered
a quick wind will push you eastward
where your rain will nourish an area already saturated
I will lie here in the west—empty and dry
hopeful that a stronger wind will return you

I am like a death row prisoner
waiting for a pardon what will not come
waiting for a stay that will never be penned
I will eat, grow fatter
counting the days until I am led away
hoping— until the very last minute
that you will come through
knowing—from the start that you will not

You are like the governor
reading a pardon that you cannot sign
pushing aside a stay that you will not grant
You will stop eating, grow thinner
counting the days until I am led away
wishing— until the very last minute
that you could come through
knowing–from the start that you cannot

SORRY...I DON'T UNDERSTAND
Jennifer D. King

Come here darling
Can you
make it
make sense?
I just can't seem to grasp (you) it.

Maybe I lack your savvy
perhaps
I'm just not sensitive enough
to catch your drift
Sorry...I don't understand.

Your method of conveying
your intention escapes me
skirting as it does
between sly innuendo
and slippery suggestion.

It's over. No. We're over
oh, that's clear enough
don't I feel silly
now that you've made it
so perfectly clear.

I wish I could be just as transparent
as you
I wish I could make others understand me
you know
read between my lines—
see through my confusion.

Don't you think
they should be able to see
how clearly
confused I am.

A DOMESTIC DISTURBANCE
Jennifer D. King

Gloria peered into the cabinet at the orderly rows of coffee cups. She reached in and pulled out a light blue cup with bright yellow sunflowers on it. Emblazoned across the top–in bold black letter, it declared EVERYTHING'S BETTER AFTER I'VE HAD MY FIRST CUP. She snorted and wondered if everything would be better after she had her first cup of coffee this morning. She wondered if anything would ever be better again.

She walked across the small kitchen and headed toward the coffeemaker. A sharp pain in her side stopped her twice. When she reached the coffeemaker, she slowly lifted the pot and poured the dark liquid into the cup. Her hands were shaking so badly that several drops missed the cup and splashed across the top of her hand. She usually added milk and three heaping teaspoons of sugar, but not this morning. She only sought the comfort of the hot liquid. Perhaps the scalding hot coffee would make her forget about last night.

Last night. Gloria had sensed Frank's presence before she saw him. A menacing coldness had suddenly filled the room, penetrating the warmth of her comforter. She had awakened from a sound sleep and sat straight up in the bed. Frank's looming presence filled the doorway to the bedroom. The night light in the hallway silhouetted his huge frame. His change had taken a toll on Frank's body. The hard muscles he had once been so proud of had been reduced to pudgy roundness.

"Fine damn thing" he bellowed. "I come home from a hard day's work, and there's not a dammed thing on the table. You tell me, Katherine, why isn't there a damned thing on my table?"

Gloria knew that answering him or trying to explain was useless. He hadn't been to work in more than seventeen years. She wasn't Katherine. Katherine was his first wife–she had died thirty-seven years ago. Instead, Gloria pressed back into the pillow while he raged on.

"You hear me, woman? What the hell good are you if I can't even come home to a hot meal?"

The pain in her side erupted again, and Gloria had to steady herself against the refrigerator. The dull throbbing in the back of her head was growing by the minute. She closed her eyes to try to stem the flow of tears that welled in her eyes. "No, dammit!" she thought. "No time for crying now."

A warm stream of tears coursed down her face. She reached up and wiped them with the back of her hand. She pushed away from the refrigerator and moved forward. After walking down the narrow hallway that connected the kitchen and living room, she had to stop and step over Frank's body.

The effort to take a wide step across the prone form of her husband sent a searing pain across her side and she spilled half of the coffee in an attempt to keep from falling. By the time Gloria reached the couch, the entire room was swaying. She was clutching her right side with her free hand and breathing through her mouth. She eased herself down on the couch, and clutching the coffee cup with both hands, she closed her eyes and prayed for the pain to subside.

Last night she had hoped–had prayed– that Frank's crazy talk would eventually stop. It hadn't. *"Get the hell outta that bed!"* Frank screamed and lumbered toward her. Gloria had scrambled out of the bed before he could reach her. She smelled liquor on his breath. She knew It was going to be bad. The doctor had told him. She had told him. Yet he continued to drink with the medications. She managed to scamper from under the covers. She had stood there cowering in the far side of the room.

"Who the hell you running from? What? You think you're too good for me to touch? My own damned wife, too good for me!" Sensing that she would try to slip past him, Frank stumbled back and blocked the doorway.

"It's been a long time since I showed you who the man is in this house. Yeah, time for me to put you in your place." Frank's hands trembled as he began to unbuckle his belt. She whimpered as she watched him slowly wind the wide leather belt around his hand, and then advance toward her.

Gloria wasn't sure how long she had been slumped on the couch. She didn't realize that she had fainted until she felt the dampness in her lap. She saw the brown coffee stain on her bathrobe and the upended coffee cup lying next to her. She was having difficulty seeing and quickly realized her left eye was closed. She reached up and felt the swelling. Her hand traveled across her face. She winced when she touched her swollen lip. Her tongue confirmed that the metallic taste in her mouth was indeed blood. She reached into her mouth, and the gentle nudging of her finger caused two of her teeth to move. When she pulled her hand away, she looked at the blood on her trembling fingers.

She had–as she always did–pleaded with him. She had begged him to let her go downstairs and heat up his meal. She knew better than to remind him that his dinner had been prepared, and had been on the table six hours ago. She knew it would only enrage him further if she pointed out that she had stayed up waiting and had only cleared the table after the Tonight Show had come on. Frank didn't say a word, and she had foolishly taken his silence for consent to move from the corner. When she reached the doorway, he had reared back. She tried to duck the approaching blow, but his belt- wrapped fist had managed to connect with the side of her head and send her sprawling onto the floor.

Through the tears in her right eye Gloria slowly surveyed the room. The glass-topped coffee table lay on its side. The crystal vase was shattered, and the ivory and violet colored wildflowers that had been so artfully arranged in it now lay broken and strewn among the shards of glass scattered across the hardwood floor. Rust-colored stains were splattered on the back and the seat of the Chesterfield chair Frank had surprised her with the chair for their anniversary. How long ago was that? She wasn't sure anymore. Five, maybe six years. Before he changed he was always bringing home gifts for her, praising her cooking, admiring how she dressed, kissing her when she least expected it. Then, he had changed. It had been a long time since he had kissed her. It felt like it had been a lifetime since he approached her for any reason other than to yell at her–to hurt her.

The acrylic painting that hung above the chair now dangled from its wire. The butter-colored wall to the right of the chair had a deep gouge in it. The wall was further defaced by bloody handprints. On the opposite wall, the oak-framed mirror Frank had given her for a wedding present was cracked. Cracked--like Frank. As she peered into the splintered mirror, Gloria's hand reached to the golf-ball sized knot in the side of her head. A chunk of her hair clung to her hand when she pulled it away.

Frank had been thrown off balance when he struck her. While he stumbled to right himself, she propelled herself through the doorway and ran for the stairs. She had tripped on the second step and went rolling down the next six. Lying there dazed--she could hear him running toward her. A pain in her side slowed her rising, and by the time she got to her feet, he was on her grabbing, ripping the back of her nightgown as she sprang from his grasp. She had thought that if she could only make it to the back door in the kitchen, she would have a chance to get out of the house.

Gloria leaned back into the sofa and marveled at how peaceful Frank's face looked. The early morning light from the window spilled across his face. From across the room, and through her one open eye, she could still see just how long and thick his lashes were. When they had first married, she told her friends that it had been his beautiful eyes and luxurious eye lashes that had first attracted her to him.

She had left one of the lower cabinet doors open, and, in the darkness, she ran into it and fell against the sink. Frank was on top of her as she tried to catch her breath. He drew back, called her "Katherine" again, and then he hit her--hard in the stomach. She had grabbled wildly at the side of the sink to keep from falling, and had turned over the drain board and sent its contents spilling across the floor. Unable to remain upright, she had gone crashing down on the floor amid the plates, glasses, and cutlery. Her thigh had landed on something cold and sharp. A butcher's knife.

Frank roared, "You can't run from me, bitch. You might as well stay still, and get what you got coming to you." She had reached under her thigh and grabbed the knife.

Frank lay on his back, and a wide red stain covered his blue chambray work shirt. A pool of blood surrounded his body and had begun to soak into the floor. The heavy leather belt was still wrapped around his right hand. The hilt of the butcher knife protruded from his throat. As another wave of nausea pressed her back into the sofa. She heard the unmistakable sounds of sirens growing closer. The police. The neighbors had heard–they always did. Sometimes, when she went out to empty the trash or work in the yard, they whispered "Hello, Gloria," and quickly averted their eyes away from her blackened eyes. If she passed them on the sidewalk, they would look over her head as they spoke. They pretended not to see the ugly bruises on her neck and arms. They were ashamed for her. None of them had ever dared come over and help her when Frank was out of control, but they could be counted on to call the police. She didn't blame them. She couldn't blame them. They didn't understand. Hell, she didn't understand.

The pounding on the front door stirred her. She sighed and pushed herself upright. She started crying again. She cried because she hurt. She cried for Frank. She cried for his children--who would tell them? How would they tell them? What would they think? "Oh my God!" Now everyone would know–everyone would think they knew. She cried even harder. No one would understand that Frank was sick--that he had changed. Frank hadn't understood that he was sick. He didn't remember that he had once loved her. The newspaper headlines would only scream the ugly part: *Elderly woman stabs 76 year old husband to death.* The pounding on the door was insistent now. As she stood, she looked down. She was still holding the coffee cup–the one that read EVERYTHING'S BETTER AFTER I'VE HAD MY FIRST CUP.

HIS SEEDS
Julaina Kleist

With no memory of him,
I, at seventeen and longing,
Insistently asked, " Mom, where is he,
The one who held me, his small baby,
In fatherly arms?"

Stubborn, she shook her proud head
And the slightly graying halo
Danced with the flow of her slenderness.
But her eyes pierced my soul as she spoke,
"On the Rural Road."

I found the farmer's old house,
Climbed cracked wooden porch steps and peeked.
A window framed the cereal box
Waiting on a table set for one
In his warm kitchen.

My surprise visit didn't
Diminish delight to see me.
Familial shyness and stilted speech,
We tried to express too much to say
When past meets present.

In bibbed overalls, he led
The way to a closed door.
Opening it, cold air engulfed us,
The guardian of a seed pile
For planting next spring.

To him the seed pyramid,
Like a necessary sculpture,
Unnoticed as unusual.
For me it was sadly curious
In the living room.

So excited to show me,
He searched a drawer filled with photos
And found in the chipped varnished bureau,
A worn picture of my mother
From long years ago.

He saved this one she had left,
And treasured it through these lost times,
His wife, the woman he still loved
But who chose not to live with him
Here on his old farm.

His stiff, work-swollen fingers
Clasped the fading snapshot. With moist
Eyes, a statue's gaze on it, he said
"Beautiful. You look just like her.
The days she lived here."

I leaned toward my father,
Snuggling as close to him as I could
And reached to connect with the big hand
That held my mother, envisioning
A timeless trio.

The deep earthy smell of him
The waft of the grain on the floor
Melded a mosaic memory
For me to have forever—
Now that he is gone.

MEMORIES OF FRANCE
Rita LaBrie

Lavender ice cream screams Provence
AND Ratataouille too

A sidewalk cafe
A priceless Monet
and a delicious kiss from you!

DEMENTIA
Rita LaBrie

Childhood fears and
unhappy memories resurface
to haunt the days and nights,

Adult trials and tribulations
take center stage
While snippets of happiness
stand patiently in the wings
Waiting their turn for an encore,

Row, row, row your boat
Life if but a dream
suddenly becomes reality
Or is life really a nightmare,

You then set sail on
the cruise of a lifetime
Drifty aimlessly around
the world in a sea of confusion.

BIRTHING NATE
Eleanor Levine

It's a bit over twenty-eight years ago that I birthed my son. Maybe because it was so long ago or that I was an "older woman," that I can look back through the lens of absurdity. Given that the reality wasn't much fun, I have decided to tell the real story of Nate's birth.

Getting to the hospital: This first step required five tries. Try 1: We forgot the bag of goodies. Try 2: I forgot to put my shoes on. Try 3: We forgot to turn off the uneaten dinner on the stove. Try 4: I forgot to call my midwife. No, I didn't have her number with me. Try 5: We made it by remembering why we were going.

Arrival: The attendant brought out a wheelchair. "For me?" I asked. "Yes, he said. "Am I injured?" "No, we do this for all patients." "But I am not sick." "Doesn't matter. It's routine." "But I can still walk. How do you think I got to the desk?" He pushed the wheelchair closer assuming I'd take the hint. "No," I said. "I may be thirty-nine, but I can still walk." "No you can't. Not once you're admitted." Wow, I thought. I didn't know paralysis went along with pregnancy but I was nice–we women are good at that in public and gave my "Yes, Sir" smile. "OK," I said, "after I sign in."

The wait: "No, your OB/GYN is not on duty tonight. Dr. Anderson will attend you." I think, hey, I had perfect attendance for a whole month in fourth grade. Am I going to get a little plastic camel or horse? Do I still get the baby? "When can we meet her?" I ask. "When she makes her rounds." "When might that be?" "Can't say," the nurse replies. So I think, but of course never said, What do you mean you can't say? Have you lost your voice? Are you forbidden to tell me? Oh, maybe you don't know? I stare at her as she keeps her frozen smile while standing in silence as if I was supposed to say, "That's OK. I can wait. I've done this so many times before that I know the routine." Am I in some horror movie? Am I in some song, like "She'll Be Coming Around the Mountain When She Comes"? Am I having a baby or a mule? Are these the thoughts of an irrational pregnant woman? No! They were my way of coping with an irrational system.

When push comes to shove: Hours later (who can remember how many, because there is never a clock in the labor room, the nurse returns.) "Hmmm, hmmm," she says running her hands around my belly. "It's time to push. You're dilated and ready to go." One hot dog coming up, my mind flashes. No mustard, yes to catsup, and hold the relish. Push? What's she talking about? Push the door open? Push the food aside? Push my fears away? Is she speaking English? Is she talking to me? No one has been talking to me for hours and suddenly I am a star. Funny, I don't feel so glamorous. "Push." "I have to go to the toilet." "Go on, it's over there," she says pointing, as if I hadn't been over there a hundred times already. "Crap," I scream, "the nurse said for me to push, not you," I say to my husband, who had a sudden urge for the bathroom. "Move over." "I can't," he says with embarrassment. "It's dribbling down my leg. I can't hold it." And I pee on the floor standing up. I can hear the nurses muttering things like, "She shouldn't have a baby at her age. No control." "What a pair, the two of them." I'm thinking, how about a towel? Or, how about you keep your mouths shut?

Coming out: "That's it, push." I hear Dr. Anderson saying. "Good girl." So now I am a dog. Good girl, good girl. That's good. You fetched the newspaper. "Push, just a little bit more. His head is showing." I'm thinking head, schmead, I cannot believe women do this more than once. "Push, he's coming. A little more. That's it. One more push." That's all I got left, lady, one more and then it's your turn.

Done: "Out. He's out," Dr. A says. "Looks healthy. Good color. We'll do a few quick tests and then you can hold him." No, can't you do some longer tests; take your time. I am tired. I have years of responsibility ahead of me. More time, please. But it's too late.

Going home: The wheelchair is back. "Policy," says a new attendant. "Hospital policy." I climb in, hoping he'll come home with me and wheel me around for the rest of my life. "Sign here, please. And here and here." The attendant reaches out for my hand and helps me out of the chair. "You are free to go." Free? Free? I decide to leave without wondering what that meant.

Home: I have no idea how to be a mother. The books I'd read are nothing compared to a hungry newborn. The midwife comes, chews

Nate's finger nails so he won't scratch himself and I won't cut off his fingers with a pair of clippers. She says he's sucking well and that my milk is good. I think, thank goodness for common sense and instincts.

The next 28 years: Immunizations, temper tantrums, birthdays, school trips, girlfriends, and graduations; it's now 29 years later.

A BIRD IN A CAGE
Nada Light

It was 6:00 p.m. In a watering hole for singles somewhere on the East Coast, workers from several large office buildings poured into "My Favorite Time" to mingle and drink after work. People were tightly packed at the bar ordering drinks. A blond rather handsome man in an Armani jacket was seated at the crowded bar talking with a very striking woman in a teal blue pantsuit. The outside door opened and a slender woman with dark hair swept up in a ponytail walked in.

"Helen, Helen. I can't believe it's you!" exclaimed Richard, the handsome blond man. He sprang from his seat and rushed over to her. "I've been thinking I should give you a call and here you are!" he said enthusiastically with a big smile and wide eyes. He reached out to hug her.

Helen was flabbergasted to see Richard unexpectedly. She took a step backward. "Oh, hello Richard," she said with some disinterest. "I am just as surprised to see you." She looked past him and saw the woman in the teal suit seated next to Richard's vacant stool. Helen continued to scan the crowd. "Why don't you go back to your friend at the bar." Helen wondered to herself, "good grief what did I ever see in this guy?"

"Wait, Helen, I'm not with her," Richard said, thinking it was a good thing that Miss Pantsuit rebuffed him. "Hold on, just give me a minute. A lot has happened in the two years since you left for your writing assignment in the Middle East. Why don't we at least have a drink together to celebrate your homecoming? I can tell you about all the changes for me when I moved to Boston." He walked back to the bar, but looked behind himself to see Helen still standing where they first saw each other. Richard walked back to her.

"See, dear Helen, I didn't forget you. I knew where you were!" Richard asserted with a smile and a wink. He seemed a little too eager to continue with his news.

"Some other time, Richard." Helen hesitated to follow him and sit at the bar. "I'm here to meet my friend, Norma. Do you remember her? By the way, she filled me in on your present life."

"Of course I remember Norma," brushing aside Helen's last comment, Richard replied with a tenacious smile. "Look, she's not here yet. We can sit a minute until she comes. I'd love to see Norma anyway. Come on. Let's sit in one of the booths where it's quieter." They both walked over to a booth. Helen took the seat opposite him to see the front door when Norma would arrive.

"Well, where was I? Oh yes, how could I forget? I had this extraordinary opportunity to develop my own company. I was at the right place at the right time. A group was looking for someone to set up and head a pharmaceutical research company; I had been in their marketing division and they approached me knowing my background. It was all very exciting and all the details just fell into place." An awkward silence lingered.

Richard smiled and in a little too "cheery" voice asked, "And how have you been?" He reached out to touch her hand, but Helen pulled it away.

"So you remembered, Richard. I got my first big assignment in the Middle East," she said with a sardonic smile. "I do remember this much, we were both excited for me. Remember how we celebrated?" Helen smiled. "We both thought it would be a six- month assignment at the most. What I didn't know was the geography. The location for the story was somewhere around the Iranian border. And we were debriefed over there and not stateside. All the turmoil at that time was in Iraq. But *Time* needed a reporter in the area where trouble was brewing. It was relatively safe when I first got there. Then things turned hostile very quickly and I was caught in a small border town with no allied troops. Several of us were captured. Maybe you read about my capture," she paused and waited to see if he had any response. Richard was busy looking at the bar's crowd. He finally looked at her face. Helen's eyes were glistening with tears for a moment. But she clenched her teeth, took a deep breath and continued. "Anyway now I'm back one month and came here to meet Norma for a drink after her work."

Richard nodded and added, "No, I didn't read about your capture. What a picnic that must have been!" He laughs at his own comment. Helen doesn't laugh.

"Richard, listen to me" she began in a demanding voice, "I was in Iran, held captive for a year! Do you get that? That's certainly nothing to laugh about. No words can really describe what it was like being held in a foreign cell. It's filth, unsafe food and water, and no toilet. I could go on but really don't want to talk about it. I've done all my talking. I went away thinking we were so much in love, but I sense that's all changed. I got one letter from you after I first arrived and sent you a reply. But then I heard nothing from you. I said to myself what's going on? Then my capture happened quickly after that. I had no chance to contact anybody. Didn't you wonder why you got no more letters? I didn't plan to be captured and tortured in Iran." She took a deep breath to compose herself and sat quietly for a moment. Helen looked down at her hands wishing that somehow she could just forget all this and move on. She thought it's all over anyway. "So I'm meeting Norma for a drink tonight," she said and moved over to stand up.

"Helen, please stay so we can talk. I came down here to have a drink with John, an old friend of mine. I had no idea you would be here. It must have been fate that we met. Let me finish about the big things that have happened to me while you were gone. I am, well to put it on the table, wealthy and on my way to becoming very wealthy. If it still works for us Helen, there could be room for you. I'm a good catch. I'm young, handsome, and RICH! "What-do-ya say? We could be a great team, you and your newfound status in journalism and me with my expertise and business success."

Helen just smiled. Trying to seem interested, she said, "The last time we saw each other you were into pharmaceuticals."

Richard nodded his head, yes. "Right now I have several pharmaceutical companies approaching me to join their research teams. They really want my patents and they can have them if they pay me well."

"Exactly what kind of research, Richard? Are you talking drug research? And can I assume you also do drug testing? I do remember they stopped human testing years ago," she said sarcastically.

" Well yes, we do some animal testing."

"Think about this drug tester, man," Helen retorted. "I was held in a cage for a year and treated like a rat. I think I was given drugs in that awful food to see what my responses would be. Maybe that was their form of "drug testing." I didn't understand what was happening, why I was always sick. I thought it was from the torture, deprivation, that awful food, and all the stress."

"Helen, Helen," he pleaded. "Please, my company doesn't do anything inhumane. We only do some live testing for really important drug development like new cancer drugs."

Helen moved out of the booth and stood up. "Richard, I am not the naïve young woman you knew before. That whole experience in Iran gave me a different perspective on lots of things in my life. You go and have fun with your money. I'm not interested in climbing into another cage, even one lined with dollar bills. My values have changed. So let's just go our separate ways. I know that is best for me. Good-bye, Richard." He watched in total bewilderment as Helen left the bar.

A TIME OF HOPE
Joy Lucadello Luster

Whenever memories are pursued down the dusty or dimmed days of the past, a special pleasure arises when a sparkle or glint is caught, like a brief flash of sunlight, and a special moment in time is recalled. July 21, 1961, when my husband was arrested in Jackson, Mississippi, as a Freedom Rider is one such moment.

I will always recall that evening when Orville left. "Daddy!" Three year-old Robbie pointed toward the small black and white television screen.

"Where? Where?" Laura, then nine, ran towards the set. "Mom, did you see?"

I nodded as she continued. "Do you think he'll have to go to jail?"

"Well, probably, but he won't be there long. The Quakers will see to it that he gets bailed out." I wiped my hands on the dishtowel, then reached over and hugged her. "He'll be all right, sweetheart. He'll be all right." I hoped that was true.

"Daddy in jail? Why?" Robbie chimed in.

I gathered both children in my arms and tried to explain again why their father was joining several people from the American Friends Service Committee as well as some others to become a Freedom Rider in the civil rights movement.

As we talked we watched the nine men, two black and the rest white, as they walked up the stairway to the airplane. One of the black men was my husband. I felt proud and admired what he was doing. At the same time, I feared for his safety.

We had been working for civil rights for many years. Orville Luster and I had married in 1949 in Fellowship Church, perhaps the only multi-racial church in the country. Dr. Howard Thurman was the minister. He had left a position as professor of religion at Howard University in Washington, D.C. to come to San Francisco and try to change what had become known as the most segregated hour of the week. He had studied for a brief time in India with Mahatma Gandhi, and gained respect in the Bay Area for his thoughtful and inspiring sermons and books. In the summer of 1949, Orville and I spent a number of hours with him as he counseled us about marriage, and especially inter-racial marriage.

Orville, a returned veteran, was enrolled at the University of San Francisco as a GI student. I was a bank teller and taking a class or two at the same time. In 1948 the state Supreme Court had ruled the miscegenation laws of the state unconstitutional, so we could marry legally. Jim Crow was active in the southern states; in California we also met discrimination. Orville had difficulty finding work. We had a hard time finding places to live, most of my family stopped speaking to me, and we suffered taunting and harassment in public on occasion.

His family became more cordial, my family relaxed a little as the years passed, and a gradual acceptance occurred.

Restrictive covenants were in force at that time, and non-whites were unable to buy homes in most areas. My sister and I had gone house hunting, since we were shown many more homes that we would have if Orville had been with us. Our first home purchase was about a block over the county line in Daly City in 1958.

We had each worked and gone to school in those early years. We were poor, had struggled, and were finally succeeding. During and through a variety of jobs, Orville applied for civil service positions. Eventually he was hired by the San Francisco Youth Guidance office and began his work with at-risk teenagers. In 1961 he was the Executive Director of the Youth for Service Agency, originally founded by the American Friends Service Committee, and now operating independently. Orville's success in his work with youth gangs in the various parts of San Francisco was gaining him local and national recognition. In his work he broke up gang clashes and helped many young men get back to school or into training programs.

We had been following the unfolding civil rights movement with keen interest. We chuckled when Rosa Parks refused to give up her seat in the white section of the bus. "Maybe it's changing," we'd say to one another. "Maybe there is hope." We felt anguish as we watched the riots and the demonstrators being clubbed and beaten.

We watched as Martin Luther King, Jr. led marches across the south. "Just think, Joy," Orville sighed, shaking his head in disbelief. "Dr. Thurman has done it again. He was actually a teacher and mentor to Dr. Martin Luther King, Jr."

"I know," I shifted to a more comfortable position on the couch, "All of those sermons we listened to while he was in the Bay Area. He taught the same philosophy when he went to Boston College."

Just about a week before that eventful trip to Jackson, Orville said, "Red Stevenson called me today and asked me to go to Mississippi. They're going to participate in some sit-ins. What do you think?"

"What do you think?" I countered, buying some time, "I think it's exciting. But dangerous!"

"I want to go." He smiled, "It won't cost us any money. The American Friends will pay for it."

"Well," I said reluctantly, "If you really want to go, then do it."

"There will be only one other black man, Reverend Banks from Ocean View." Orville laughed. "I think some of those other black preachers didn't feel they could take the time."

While Orville was away I tried to keep our regular household routine. Laura went to school in the morning, carrying her lunch and books. I took Robert to Ocean View Co-op nursery school for three hours. Sometimes I'd stay and help with the children. On other days, I would shop or wash clothes, or do the many tasks that seemed to always be there. On Tuesday and Thursday evening we all went to the accordion school down on Junipero Serra Boulevard where Laura was taking lessons. Robbie and I would wander up and down the street to look in the furniture store and the ski and sports store while we waited. Inside, I felt hollow, as if a part of me had been spirited away to hide in one of those fairy tale forests. Would I escape the ogre? Was Orville all right? Why were people so hateful and mean? No, don't go there, I told myself. Take care of your children. Help make them strong and capable. Do not give into fear. So the days passed.

One Wednesday the phone rang and I ran to answer. "Joy, I'm out of jail." The unseen burden strapped to my back lifted, and I felt light and giddy.

"How are you? When will you be home? How was it?" I tumbled the questions out like a reckless gambler at the roulette table tosses out dice.

"Well, those guys want to go to Montgomery, Alabama, next. It wasn't too good, but I'll tell you all about it when I get home. They arranged bail just this morning. I wanted to tell you that I am all right."

We talked some more for awhile. "I'll let you know when I am coming home," he said.

Two days later in the middle of the afternoon a car stopped out front. I saw Orville get out and the car drive away. I ran down the stairs and opened the door. "Thank God!" We hugged and kissed, and we clung to each other.

After another hug, Orville asked, "Where are the kids? Are they o.k.?"

"They're fine. Robbie is across the street at the Rogers' and Laura should be home from school soon."

Our emotions subsided, and he began to talk, his speech still carrying the soft patterns of his native Oklahoma. "First we went to Tuskegee. We slept in some kind of dormitory. Early the next day, we met Dr. King. That was a great honor. We were in this classroom, and he spoke to us about what he was doing and his hopes for the movement. He is a very compelling person. Looks just like he does on TV." Orville leaned back on the kitchen chair and stretched his long legs. "He stressed the non-violent aspects of the sit-ins and told us to be sure to follow the procedures." His brown face broke into a smile, "You'd better believe it, I wasn't about to physically fight bare-handed against those police and their long billy clubs, and neither was anyone else."

"So, what happened next?"

"Well, these instructors came in. They told us how to curl up if they start beating you, how to go limp, stuff like that." Orville went to the refrigerator and took out a bottle of orange juice. I handed him a glass.

"Then that night we went to Jackson. We stayed in these people's homes before we went to jail. They assigned me to stay with this old white lady. She was nice, but I sure was uncomfortable. I didn't sleep much, waiting for someone to knock on the door in the middle of the night and haul me out. I was there two nights."

He took a swig of the juice, gulping it down. "We met with some other demonstrators and we walked around a little, and decided where we should sit-in. Made me nervous. Black and white people walking up the street together drew a lot of angry looks. I have to hand it to those Quakers; they just didn't give a damn about what those other white people said to them. "

"Next day we staged a sit-in at a local store. We didn't resist, and we weren't hurt when they arrested us for disturbing the peace."

"How was the jail?" I asked.

"Well, the jail was awful," he began, "the white guys got put into better, cleaner cells, and they were well treated. That's what they told us later, anyway. But Steve Banks and I were put into the Negro cells. Dirty." He winced, and I was reminded of how immaculate he liked to be. "And the food was slop. What we couldn't eat, we flushed down the toilet so they wouldn't serve it to us again. They threw stained mattresses on the floor. There were no blankets, sheets or anything. A toilet with no lid or seat was in the corner of the cell. Then there was a lot of crap we had to listen to. Oh, I'm so glad to be home."

"What about Montgomery? Did you go there?"

"Yeah, we all got on a bus and rode from Mississippi to Alabama. A bunch of sheriff deputies were waiting when we arrived. They all sort of looked like Bull Connors. And they all carried sticks about three feet long. When we got off the bus, they started following us. Steve and I decided that we didn't want to be in any more jails. So we said goodbye to the other guys and headed for the airport."

Orville pulled at the front of his blue shirt and stood up, "I've got to unpack and take a shower." He picked up his suitcase and headed for the bedroom.

I looked into the refrigerator to see what I could cook for dinner. It had to be special. This was going to be a celebration. I felt happy. It was a time of hope.

GETTING READY
Joy Lucadello Luster

"We best start thinking about getting ready," Papa was saying. "Going to Californy isn't as dangerous as it used to be a few years back. These Bidwell people know the best wagon party routes."

Lide drew the blue and yellow quilt around her shoulders and leaned over slightly to peer down from the children's loft into the kitchen below. Papa was standing and brushing Mama's long brown hair, moving his large, work-worn hands gently. "Sarah, I know you have some doubts. Brother Ben has bought land and the older ones seem to be doing all right. But for you and me, the war is long over, and its 1873 already. I truly believe we'd best make a new start. His voice dropped and Lide strained to hear. "Sarah, maybe I'll find you one of those leftover gold nuggets for you to wear on a chain around your neck."

Her mother giggled, "Squire, we best be getting to bed now."

Lide listened to the familiar sounds as her parents turned the damper on the fire, checked the wooden latch across the door, then entered their bedroom and softly closed the door. She snuggled down into the bedding, hugged her rag doll and thought about the strange conversation.

The first chance Lide had to ask anyone about what she had heard was the following morning when she and her sister Deborah were getting water from the well. "Deb, what's Californy, and how do we get ready?"

Deborah lowered the bucket. "Lide, I'm not supposed to talk about it, so hush."

"Why, is it something awful?" Lide's blue eyes grew round with anxiety at this thought. She patted her ankle-length dress with quick little gestures, and dug the toe of her boot into the slushy snow and mud which surrounded the well.

"Lide," Deborah spoke with the superiority of an eight year old, "It's not awful, exactly. You're not supposed to know because you are too young and you blab everything. So just hush! Help me turn this wheel and don't stand there asking silly questions."

In the days that followed everything seemed the same as usual. It was winter time, so Papa and the boys didn't go out is the fields much.

Mostly, they fixed things. They mended broken harness, and they went to the blacksmith to get new farm tools or to repair the old ones. They took care of the horses and chopped wood for the stove. Mama cooked, mended and sewed on her quilt. Lide waited and waited for someone to tell her more. She had just about given up.

Then one Sunday as they were finishing dinner, Papa said, "Children, your Ma and I have decided to move to Californy. We've got to be ready by the time of the spring thaw."

Her brothers, Jim and Lane, grinned broadly at each other, and Deborah looked into her lap and poked at a broken fingernail.

"Crops haven't been too good the last couple of years. I've lived here in Hancock County, Illinois, all of my life, but now your mother and I feel it's time to move on. Just like the old folks did when they came here from Indiana and Ohio." Papa's gaze fell upon Lide, "You'll have to start acting like a big girl now, Lide, and learn to take care of yourself, and you will be helping with baby, Dade. Deb can work with your mother on getting the household goods in order."

Lide lowered her eyes, her mind racing. Getting ready had something to do with going away. Why did they have to move? She felt proud that she was big enough to take care of herself. After all, she was three and a half years old. Her eyebrows puckered, not sure if she was happy or sad.

As the children were excused from the table, Sarah Thomas spoke, "Redd up the table, girls, and let's get started with those dishes." She smiled as the girls worked to straighten the kitchen.

"Girls," she continued, "We're going to be traveling a long ways in a wagon train with other families. We can't take everything with us. We'll be leaving the big pieces of furniture. Each of you can bring just one thing to play with." Her needle went in and out of the blue and green cloth squares, making fine small stitches as she spoke. "Lide, you'll have to decide whether you want your doll or your little hobby horse that Papa made for you. Deborah, you may bring your book and one toy. We'll be moving to a new farm, and Papa feels that out west will be right nice for us."

Lide was bursting with excitement, "Mama, are we leaving right now?"

"No, child, it will be in about a month. Meantime, we're going to decide what to take and what to leave behind. We have to get ready." Uncle Ben would take some of the livestock. He and his family owned land and would not be leaving, she explained. "Just our family is leaving."

A few days later they traveled to Stillwell County. This time it was to say goodbye to Sarah's relatives. Sitting around the spacious table after dinner, they spoke of how old Hiram Stillwell had been born on the East Coast in 1796. Grandpa recalled how his mother, Sarah Morgan, and his father married in Kansas. Grandpa At (Arthur) Stilwell was their second son, born in 1825. Lide's grandmother Deborah Cline was his first wife. After she died he had moved to southern Illinois and married again. Lide had heard many of the stories before, but she enjoyed being allowed to sit and listen as the grownups talked.

Squire and Sarah's decision to move West meant that they would need to leave some of their household goods and some farm equipment with the Stillwell relatives. The women cooked and baked and Lide felt that it was just like a party. Everyone received gifts. There were hand-knit wool scarves, bonnets, and for Papa, a new crow bar. He allowed that it would come in mighty handy especially while they were on the trail. As they left there were tearful goodbyes and promises to take care of one another.

The following weekend the Thomas family came to say goodbye. Papa liked to tell the story of how his father had been born in New Jersey around 1800, had traveled some, married Margaret Deborah Caterline in Butler, Ohio, and eventually moved to Illinois in the 1830's. As Papa told his children, "I've been born and bred in Illinois."

Squire valued his older bother's opinion, and he and Ben spent much of that day discussing the move while the women fixed the food for the dinner. Lide thought Uncle Ben was rather gruff, but he was always willing to ride the girls on his knee while he sang 'Yankee Doodle Dandy." He would lift his leg high in the air when he got to the last line, and then abruptly lower his heavy boot. They would squeal with delight as they tumbled down his shin to the floor. More gifts and tearful goodbyes were exchanged later in the evening before Ben and his family finally drove the carriage down the long dirt road leading away from the house.

Deborah and Lide were getting very excited. Californy was far away, but they thought it would be fun to travel and not have to do their regular chores. Maybe they could ride the horses, just like the boys. They would have to ask Papa, because Mama probably wouldn't think it was very ladylike. They wondered if they would see Indians and buffalo and mountain lions.

When she talked with Deborah, Lide felt good about going to a new place. When she was alone, however, she worried. Would there be friends for her in Californy? Where would she sleep? Would Papa remember to make a new hobby horse to replace the one she was leaving? Would she be able to look after Baby Dade the way Papa had asked? Sometimes she thought it had been better when she was the baby. Then she didn't have to be responsible.

On that special morning, while the sky was still dark and only a faint paleness in the east was visible, they wakened with anticipation and excitement. The blankets were rolled and stored in the already laden wagon. They had a breakfast of ham slices, bread, milk, and Sarah's canned peaches.

Papa said rather gruffly, "You boys ride the two extra horses. Your Mama and me will be driving the wagon. Lide and Deborah, get in the front part of the wagon so we can keep an eye on you." Baby Sedalia was already asleep in the small crib that was roped to the inside of the wagon so that it would not move.

He helped the girls clamber into the wagon, and then got up onto the seat. "Well, Sarah, I guess the time is now." He flicked the reins and the horses started to slowly move. Squire Thomas didn't look back. He didn't look at Sarah. Lide always remembered the set of his jaw, and how his hand came up to wipe his forehead, pushing his hat up. He put his hat back in place, crushing down the straight brown hair, "Giddyup, damn you horses!"

Lide, clutching the rag doll Mama had made for her, tried to see past her sister, as Deborah craned her neck towards the house. It had always been home, and it was a little scary to be leaving it forever. Sarah didn't look, but she kept wiping her eyes for a long time.

Note: My maternal grandmother, Ellen Eliza Thomas (sometimes known as Ella or Lide) was born in Illinois on June 6, 1869. My great-grandfather, Squire Thomas, moved his family to northern California when Lide was still three years old. This is how it may have happened.

WOMAN
Joy Lucadello Luster

A woman curls long hair, teasing and backcombing,
wraps it carefully in a scarf.
Expression

A woman dresses in mini skirts, dyes her hair in two colors,
purple and blue.
Regression

A woman weeps, brushes rouge to her cheeks,
pulling a lock over the bruise by her eye.
Depression

A woman, eyes half-closed, watches a young beauty
carelessly smile and toss her head.
Succession

STORIES AND TALES
Jessie McElroy - Thrash

She heard his music
Strumming, picking and plucking
Stories and tales
of lost innocence
lost love
Stories and tales
bold adventures
of walking the vast planet
Stories of random thinking
Tales of countless possibilities
She heard his music
Strumming, picking and plucking
Stories and tales

SUNDAY CHURCH TRAIN
Jessie McElroy - Thrash

Sunday, the T train is no ordinary train
it could be called the Sunday Church Train
devoid of the students, businessmen and researchers
the Sunday Church Train rolls on
many places of worship are visible
some well established
made of brilliant stone or brick
some with steeples and ample parking spaces
others new or not so new
store fronts, renovated cafes or bars
not well lit

The faces on the way are mostly animated
anticipating hearing the Good News
the dress is Sunday best
Sunday best
a well worn shiny red pin stripe suit with tattered cuffs
a shiny faded brown suit that has lost its luster
and no longer fits.
missing buttons
on a way too long dressy overcoat
new shoes old shoes all spiffy shined
torn clothe shoes
A lady with well tailored Usher Board suit naming her church

This Sunday train is transportation
for the animated faces to hear the Good News.
news that help is on the way
some way their God will provide all their needs
love and acceptance always there for the asking

The Sunday Church Train rolls on

IMAGINATION
Jessie McElroy-Thrash

What about imagination
A thing that's created from and
Out of the mind
Where does it come from
Is it real or only imagined

Imagine no place to sleep
Few clothes to wear
No food to eat
Imagine no job for years
No signs of hope
Too many tears

What about imagination
A thing that's created from and
Out of the mind
Where did that come from
Is it real or only an imagination

IT'S ALMOST HERE
Jessie McElroy-Thrash

It's almost here again
It–long gusty cold nights
It–lost freedom
It–short sunless colorless days

Each year
It loses some sting, mystery
New skills learned, cultivated
Mind becomes less restless, more thankful
Body responds with new energy

Each year
It will return
Sting and mystery will remain
Mind and body responding with
More thankfulness
Accepting all nights and days

MOSIAC HOME
Sally A. Miller

The year was 1956. Mom and Dad were separated and Mom, my sister and I moved into Grandma's house in Plainville, Connecticut. Gram explained, to my dismay, that the three of us would live in the *cabin* in the back of the property during the summer. We would share Gram's house in the front of the property in the winter. I was devastated. You see, most of my new friends in town had homes just like the home on the *Leave it to Beaver* show that we watched on Thursday evening. That home had two parents, lots of love and beautiful surroundings.

Despite my apprehension, life in the cabin that summer was Grrrrrrreat! Although the three of us were crowded into a one-room cabin that had been divided into two rooms, I now realize that it was one of the most precious times in my life.

The summer was a magical time – a quiet time – a time to listen to the earth. My sister and I would wake to the sound of bacon sizzling and crackling on the stove. The smell of pine trees dampened by the morning mist mingled with the sound of bees assaulting the honeysuckle bush on the side of the cabin. Varieties of birds sang; each trying to outdo the other. The morning sun gently pried apart the tree branches to quietly steal its way into the tree-shaded yard. The rays of sun then danced across the blades of grass as if in celebration of a new day.

Once we were out of bed, we had choice of either walking up to Gram's house to use the bathroom facilities or resorting to the old outhouse in the back of the cabin. Surprised at ourselves, we chose the outhouse … you see this was just like camping out.

There was an antiquated brick-colored water pump on the side of the cabin and my sister and I would argue about which one of us would bring in the water from pump. We loved doing this chore. The thrill of that chore was to pour water into the pump to prime or start the water flowing. We would pump the handle up and down vigorously until the first blast of cold sparkling water emerged from the spout. We then put our mouths to the spout and water as fresh and cold as new fallen snow would cascade down our throats.

We would bring the water to the breakfast table, which was an old weather-beaten picnic table situated under an umbrella of pine trees. Dried pine needles plunged from the trees and decorated our breakfast table. The needles then gently fell into the bowls of freshly picked pinecones that was our table decoration. As we devoured our breakfast, our own private symphony would begin. The orchestra consisted of squirrels snapping branches as they jumped from limb to limb. The drone of bees joined in as they hovered over sweet alyssum. Dragonflies held conversations while perched on blue morning glories, which trellised up the side of the cabin, the sweet shrill of blue jays chattering at one another and the great songster herself, Ms. Red Red Robin carried the majestic harmony of the morning sonata.

Every minute or so, tiny acorns softly touched the earth as they fell from the great and mighty oak, barely missing the brown chipmunks who rattled twigs and leaves as they scurried under oak leaves. Most of the time, the only thing we heard was the soft melodic sound of nature and whispering of poems my Robert Frost recited by Mom during breakfast.

Later, I came to realize the magnificence and splendor of our life in the cabin! It was a mosaic home full of love, our own small family of women, beautiful and memorable surroundings, and most of all, wonderful, lasting memories.

Thanks Mom.

PART ONE: LIVING IN THE PRESENT
Gayle Mohrbacker

Redolent in sunshine, this grizzled Yoda redwood tree prevails in the middle of a winding street I walk to catch the bus to San Francisco. Coming back, I'll walk downhill, deep breathing its scent as I pass. No matter how good a time I've had with my children in San Francisco, I'm always eager to return to my Oakland neighborhood's greenery and birdsong and this charming little building with stucco arches and white rose bush, whose fragrance amazes, as does its ability to endure.

From within my building, shared aromas of toast, eggs, butter melting in a cast iron pan. The building next door shares cozy sounds ~~ use of spoons, plates being taken from a cupboard, kitchen chairs carefully pulled and pushed. Sometimes, a conversation in Vietnamese wafts in with fragrance of anise stars in soup, taking me back to the Summer 1967.

Daddy had brought me across the Bay to start classes at UC Berkeley. Berkeley's warm sunshine was a surprise. We knew where nothing was off-campus; we wandered down Telegraph Avenue and wound up at Caffé Mediterraneum. "I'll bet these people think I'm a professor." This was the happiest I'd ever heard my father sound. Daddy had a coffee with cream; I had a glass of milk.

Khánh might have been there that afternoon and seen us. A week or so later, still June though, he came to the marble table where I was ensconced with homework and a second espresso which I was trying to train myself to like. He smiled and asked to sit down. "Can you guess where I come from?"

He introduced me to the delicious relief of cappuccino. No more forced march ingestion of espresso for me!

During one of our many early conversations at Caffé Mediterraneum, he slapped my fingers because they were inky. He was laughing, but the slap really stung.

We had a baby, a son conscientiously happy. And quickly another baby, a daughter who climbed trees at night, rode anger to the center of the earth, and saved friends' lives.

Marriage and the way Vietnamese men miss Vietnam when they are somewhere else made us part. Khánh went back to Vietnam but was bitterly disillusioned by all Ho Chi Minh's people did after their victory in April 1975. He escaped in a boat and wound up in Houston.

He died suddenly. Thirteen years after we'd last seen each other. His voice remains my favorite sound in the world, except for our son, soon to be forty years old, playing trumpet.

All the while, I felt Khánh might drive up to the curb at my house with his belongings. I'd moved to Minneapolis. He'd seemed near. He was in Houston, only a thousand miles downstream from me.

Part Two: For Marsha

We were good friends quickly, making green tea ice cream in her kitchen just a week after we met. Talking together, we didn't have to try to boil down what we wanted to say the way other people expected us to do.

We did a lot of recreational theorizing about human nature. We were suggestible; just looking together at the bottle of Danish Kijafa liqueur in her refrigerator door made us feel festive; but usually, carried away by topic after topic, we'd forget to pour and drink any.

At the time we met, we were feeling orphaned by the men who'd left us. They were well-read intellectuals without theories of their own. So their opinions were strong and they protected them with silence. And then they left.

Another thing we had in common: We were daughters of mothers who'd had to struggle around the pitfalls of their husbands' ways. Marriage froze our mothers' spontaneity into surreptitious agility. To keep their homes going, they had constantly to outwit their men without hurting their pride.

My friend and I were gurgling streams of consciousness, with rocks to grab with our toes so that we did what needed doing in daily life. We accused ourselves of not finishing things that would've made us officially accomplished.

It was another world twelve years ago when we met. You could not find green tea ice cream anywhere except at a restaurant where they gave you just one scoop for $3.95. Now, green tea everything is everywhere. Now, even my friend and I have computers.

Once we were out of bed, we had a choice of either walking up to Gram's house to use the bathroom facilities or resorting to the old outhouse in the back of the cabin. Surprised at ourselves, we chose the outhouse... you see this was just like camping out.

There was an antiquated brick colored water pump on the side of the cabin and my sister and I would argue about which one of us would bring in the water from the pump. You see we loved doing this chore. The thrill of that chore was to pour water into the pump to prime it (start the water). We would vigorously pump the handle up and down until the first blast of cold sparkling water emerged from the spout. We then put our mouths to the spout and water as fresh and cold as new fallen snow would cascade down our throats.

We would bring the water to the breakfast table, which was an old weather-beaten picnic table situated under an umbrella of pine trees. Dried pine needles plunged from the trees and decorated our breakfast table. The needles then gently fell into the bowl of freshly picked pinecones that was our table decoration. As we devoured our breakfast, our own private symphony would begin. The orchestra consisted of squirrels snapping branches as they jumped from limb to limb. The drone of bees joined in as they hovered over sweet alyssum. Dragonflies held conversations while perched on blue morning glories, which trellised up the side of the cabin, the sweet shrill of blue jays chattering at one another and the great songster herself, Ms. Red Red Robin carried the majestic harmony of the morning sonata.

Every minute or so, tiny acorns softly touched the earth as they fell from the great and mighty oak, barely missing the brown chipmunks who rattled twigs and leaves as they scurried under oak leaves. Most of the time, the only thing we heard was the soft melodic sound of nature and the whispering of poems by Frost recited by Mom during breakfast.

I later came to realize the magnificence and splendor of our life in the CABIN! It was a mosaic home full of love, our own small family of women, beautiful and memorable surroundings, and most of all, wonderful, lasting memories.

Thanks, Mom.

GRANDMA WINNIE'S HANDS
Khaleedah Muhammad

I used to ask myself, "why me?" But when I reflect on my ancestors and family history, I have to say, "Why not me! After all, I come from generations of strong women."

The school bell rang at 3:00 p.m. I jumped out of my seat and ran to the playground to meet my two sisters. Every day we would meet in the school yard after school and race home together. As usual, I was the fastest and arrived home first. Every day we would race home to see what Grandma Winnie was cooking for dinner and dessert. I opened the front door and was immediately greeted by the heavenly aroma of her melt-in-your- mouth, twin peak cupcakes. This is just one of the many pleasurable memories I have of my maternal great-grandmother, my Grandma Winnie.

I was raised in a house with three generations of strong women, all working together. My mom worked for the Veterans Administration; my grandmother worked as a live in housekeeper; and my Great Grandma Winnie stayed home and took care of me, my two sisters, and the house. She cleaned the house, washed the clothes, shopped for groceries and maintained the household. My Grandma Winnie loved to cook and she prepared all the meals. The house was always warm, cozy and radiating with aromas of her culinary genius.

Our house was always visited by Grandma Winnie's children and loved ones and neighbors. Everyone loved her, and would come to her for advice and encouragement. She would take in family members from the South that came to seek peace and their fortunes in California. I remember when she would get her pension checks. She would take me and my sisters with her to cash her check and go shopping. Grandma Winnie would buy us our favorite hamburgers from a restaurant on 14th Street.

She was tall and stately, and had long beautiful gray hair with streaks of black hair. She had sharp features small lips and beautiful cocoa butter-colored skin. Her eyes were kind and caring, yet strong and enduring. As a young child, Grandma Winnie was my pillar of strength.

Grandma Winnie was born in Texas in 1893. She would often tell us stories her parents had shared with her about of the "slave days." She told me that her mother was a slave and her father a full bloodied Sioux Indian. I would often wonder how they got together. Later, in high school, I read that during slavery, some Indians fell in love and married runaway slaves. I wondered if her mother had been a runaway slave and thought to myself, "If she was, she probably had a better life living with her husband than having to continue being a slave." I was proud that she had the courage to run away.

Both Grandma Winnie's parents died when she was in her early teens, leaving her to raise her brothers and sisters. She married at a young age and began to have her own children. When her mother died she told me that it was she who continued to breast feed her baby sister along with her daughter. When her husband died unexpectedly, Grandma Winnie was left to raise her children as well as her brothers and sisters. Years later she would marry twice again and she gave birth to more children. I never knew much about her husbands. Like so many families, there are facts and names that just seem to disappear.

When my great uncle Gentry, her oldest son, moved to California to begin his military service, he sent for Grandma Winnie and his sisters and brothers. After he died she raised his young daughter Althea. Her other son, my great uncle Richard, found work in the shipyards; however, he died at a young age. Grandma Winnie was left to raise his son, Richard Jr.

My mother told me that during that time, when someone got sick with a communicable disease such as tuberculosis, their doctor would send them to a sanitarium in a warmer climate, like Livermore, to rest and heal. When her daughter, my grandmother, was diagnosed with tuberculosis, Grandma Winnie stepped in and continued to help raise my mother, until my grandmother was allowed to return home. I tried to count the number of children and family members Grandma Winnie raised, or helped to raise, but could never get a precise number.

Grandma Winnie never realized that she would be a witness and an active participant in the history and struggles of the Civil Rights Movement. In 1906, a charismatic Civil Rights leader, Reverend M.J. Divine, better known as Father Divine, and his wife came to California to establish the Churches of The Peace Mission Movement in the Bay Area. Father Divine wanted to prove that a man is a man, and not a color, creed or race. He preached his mission of peace and unity and administered to the poor and needy across the nation. Although I was very young, I vividly remember going with Grandma Winnie to the Father Divine's Peace Mission on the corner of 8th Street in West Oakland.

The building looked to be an old store front that had been converted to a dining and assembly hall. All the sisters at the mission were dressed in all white blouses, and they wore long skirts with white home-made aprons draping down the front. One of their mottos was, "to greet all mankind with salutation of peace." I remember entering the beautifully decorated dining room and seeing the gigantic color picture of Father and Mother Divine hanging on the wall. There were at least fifty round tables draped with sparkling white tablecloths, starched and ironed to perfection. In the center of each table was a bud vase with a single flower. Everything was beautiful, white, and clean.

What I remember most about attending those meetings was the smell of the golden brown fried chicken; mashed potatoes, salad, homemade yeast dinner rolls, and cake. There was always a flurry of activity in the kitchen. The sisters would be in there just cooking away, singing and frying chicken. Other sisters were busy in the assembly room getting ready for the services. It was such a safe and comfortable environment. Grandma Winnie appeared to know everyone there, and had been a member for many years.

When the services were over, the dining room doors were open to those who had attended the service and to anyone in need from the community.

My mother went with Grandma Winnie to the mission, and she told me that supporters and the people who could afford to pay only paid fifteen cents for fried chicken dinners. Thinking back, it was a dignified way to serve the needy. It was beautiful to see everyone eating and enjoying fellowship in such a beautiful environment.

My Grandma Winnie was a faithful follower and spent many years cooking and ministering to the needy with Father Divine's International Peace Movement Ministry.

I often wondered about Grandma Winnie's younger days. Did she have fun? Was she popular, or did she just spend all her time raising relatives' children? I know she liked to dress up when she was younger because my mother gave me a picture of her in an exquisite fur coat and a lovely silk embroidered dress. She was beautiful and looked like she was on her way to party.

Grandma Winnie had a big fluffy feather bed that I loved to bounce on when she wasn't at home or was in the kitchen. Over the years, we would have many "discussions" about her bed and her room. She also was an expert seamstress and made beautiful quilt. She was always up early in the morning, cooking, drinking her coffee and planning her day. Grandma Winnie was fond of saying that it was "the early bird that catches the worm."

There were so many things that Grandma Winnie taught me and my sisters. I remember watching her soak the white clothes in bluing. She taught us that this would keep the linens bright. She would do this before washing them in our old-fashioned wringer washer. She taught us how to sprinkle the clothes with water before ironing them in order to make the wrinkles come out easier. And then there was her cooking. I thought Grandma Winnie could cook anything. She would use only the freshest produce that she purchased from the produce truck that came to our neighborhood once a week. She would insist that we had fresh fruits and vegetables every day.

Grandma Winnie spent most of the summer canning fruits and vegetables, and she could even pickle watermelon rinds. She taught us how to select fresh meats and vegetables by taking us shopping at the Housewife's Market in downtown Oakland. My sister would spend hours in the kitchen with Grandma Winnie watching her cook and receiving cooking lessons from her. Today that sister is a gourmet cook as well as creator and founder of a seasoning salt company. My sister is known for her culinary and artistic skills.

Grandma Winnie instilled a sense of community, responsibility, and family values in all of us. She not only taught us, but she showed us that we have a duty and obligation to learn from, and help others in need. Grandma Winnie believed that each of us is indeed our brother's and sister's keeper.

Late one night, when I was nine years-old, I was suddenly awakened by the sounds of hearing my mother, grandmother and other relatives crying hysterically. I jumped out of my bed, ran to Grandma Winnie's room. I heard her say, "It's time and I am so tired!" Those were her last words. At the age of ninety-two, and after spending over seventy- eight years of her life raising her siblings and her children, grandchildren, and great-grand children, God called Grandma Winnie to rest.

For years after Grandma Winnie passed, I would go with my mother when she would deliver food, money and other necessities to her family, friends and to anyone in need. It made me understand that Grandma Winnie's legacy would continue to live on throughout the generations.

THOUGHTS
Khaleedah Muhammad

Sitting here thinking – Thoughts
Thoughts, Thoughts, Thoughts,
Knowing that thoughts are powerful
and make things happen!
and provide the driving force for achieving goals - momentum
She thought about being a singer and
is now singing all over the Bay Area.
She thought about being a writer!
and is now, A bestselling author!
Positive Thoughts combined with Faith and Perseverance
Make Things Happen!
She wanted to get a college degree, after having four children, and prayed
God Opened the way!
She just wanted to Heal after the death of her beloved husband.
God Opened the Way!
And Blessed her with children who wrapped her in love and support!
They just wanted to find good life long mates
God Opened the way!
And, they recently celebrated their thirty-seven year anniversary
No thought is too large or small and is nurtured and activated in the
MIND
REMEMBER!
"Be ye transformed by the renewing of the mind."
"As A Man Thinketh-so is he"

SAND PEBBLES
Khaleedah Muhammad

Beloved
This time is ours
There's no one in the world but us
Let's enjoy the fragrance of nature
Walk along the beach
Feel the sand between our toes
Gather exotic sea shells, rocks

Reminisce about all the wonderful and exciting times we've had together.
Life has been amazing and wonderful for us
This is our time and space
Our love will endure throughout all eternity

SERITA'S JOURNEY
Khaleedah Muhammad

Serita was born and raised in West Oakland. Her mother's family was part of the large migration of African Americans from the South to the Bay Area, looking to find better opportunities for their families as well as employment in the railroad and ship yards. Her mother told her that when her family came to West Oakland in 1912, the community was comprised of beautiful mansions that were owned by Italian and Portuguese immigrants who had also migrated to the Bay Area. As the African Americans moved into the area, the Italians and Portuguese moved out to other areas in the community, and rented their homes to African Americans. West Oakland was a wonderful place to grow up. The community operated on the "It takes A Village Theme," and everyone knew everyone and looked out for each other.

Serita's mom wanted the best education for her children. She worked overtime, sold Christmas cards, candles and anything else to make extra money so she could send Serita and her two sisters to private school. Serita and her sisters were raised as Lutherans and enrolled in the Lutheran School when Serita was in the third grade. The school was located on the church property, and had five classrooms which divided the grades from kindergarten to the 8th grade. There was also a large auditorium, social hall and kitchen upstairs.

Serita had many friends at the school. Most of the other children lived in other more affluent parts of Oakland. You could count the number of African American children on two hands. Because of the small class size, everyone knew everyone and how they were doing academically. Serita was young, full of life and ready to face the world.

Serita was nine years old and in the fourth grade when he came into her life. His name was Mr. Sylvester, and he taught fourth, fifth and sixth grade classes. To Serita, he appeared to be a giant, over 10 feet tall. She would imagine "Jack in the Bean Stalk," and in her imagination, Mr. Sylvester would be cast as the evil giant. He was a hard taskmaster and demanded excellence from the students, especially the Black students. Serita worked hard to prove herself worthy of his approval; however, no matter how hard she tried, it would never be enough. He seemed to always find ways of making her feel dumb.

One day Mr. Sylvester was leading a discussion about Africa. Serita was always intrigued and had a persistent curiosity about Africa and the people who lived there. The large map of Africa was displayed on the blackboard in the back of the classroom. The map looked to Serita to be old, intriguing and dark. Africa was a different world, a world that she didn't know anything about. She couldn't understand why the map was divided into Asia Major and Asia Minor and what kind of people lived there. All she had seen of Africa was in *Tarzan* movies, but she wasn't content to accept the fact that Africans were savages. She didn't know that much about slavery, except that Grandma Winnie had told her that her mother was an African slave, and her father was a full-blooded Sioux Indian. Grandma Winnie's parents died soon after slavery was abolished, leaving her to raise her siblings.

Mr. Sylvester had told Serita many times that she just asked too many questions. Sometimes he would ignore her raised hand and refuse to call on her. One day the class was discussing Africa, and Mr. Sylvester called Serita up in front of the class. Serita was thrilled and thought that he was finally giving her a chance to be acknowledged. Maybe she would even get answers to some of the questions that she had been thinking about for days. She strutted up to the front of the classroom and began asking questions.

Mr. Sylvester looked down at her, right in her eyes, and said," Serita, do you know what your problem is?" Serita swallowed and said, "No." He went on, "You have an inferiority complex." All the students in the room started laughing while she was thinking to herself, "What is that?" Serita had an idea of what inferior meant because Mr. Sylvester often referred to the people in Africa as inferior. She knew that whatever "inferior" was, it meant that she was not as good as others.

Serita's eyes filled with tears as she raced back to her seat and buried her head on the desk–her heart and spirit was crushed. Mr. Sylvester turned to the class and cruelly said, "Now class, let's continue." And with that he called on Sally, the smartest girl in the room to read a report that she had written about Africa. When Sally finished reading her report, Mr. Sylvester began to praise her as if she was a Nobel Prize winning orator.

Serita's mind was racing with negative thoughts and began to be filled with self doubts. She knew that if she told her mother what Mr. Sylvester told her she would really be in trouble. After all he was the teacher and knew everything. So, she promised herself that she would never tell anyone what happened. But, there was still a problem. She didn't know what the heck an "inferiority complex" was.

Later that evening, while everyone was sitting and eating at the kitchen table, Serita excused herself and went into the room she shared with the older sister. She took the dictionary from the bookshelf and looked up the word, " inferior." Her heart began to sink. Was Mr. Sylvester right? Was she inferior? Serita heard her sister coming, so she just slammed the dictionary shut, and ran past her sister back into the kitchen. She thought to herself that she would never again think herself smart, or even attempt to compete with other students. Her self confidence was devastated.

After this experience, school was never again the same for Serita. Mr. Sylvester had succeeded in shutting her up, she no longer asked questions–especially about things she didn't understand. She was no longer confident about her abilities, and it appeared to her that everyone else was smarter. What made it even worse was that some of her classmates began to tease her and call her dumb. But in spite of her feelings of inferiority, she graduated!

Serita began to learn how to channel her energies away from academics and found recognition and solace in being the social butterfly; however, she continued to be plagued with feelings of self doubts. She knew that she would eventually have to face the music academically because her mother and family expected all the children to attend college. This was not an option. African American children were expected to attend college and were taught by their parents that they had to have a good education in order to compete and be successful in the world. This was the way to elevate the whole race. Her sisters were both A students, so she had to compete with them along with peers and other students in the college prep classes she was taking in high school. She never thought she could get all A's and B's and just resigned herself to only be an average student when she graduated.

As the years passed, Serita would often ask herself, "If you don't know where you came from, how do you know where you're going, or what you can accomplish?" She realized that in order to free herself, she would have to come face to face with her feelings or continue to be a prisoner of her thoughts. She began a journey of introspection and analysis, and discovered that by sharing her feelings and fears with her loved ones, she could begin to gain greater insight. She also began to research and answer the questions that had plagued her since childhood. She discovered the Black Moors of the noble Senegal Empire, the great empires of Ghana, Mali, Timbuktu and Songhay, as well as other great African kings, queens and empires. Why didn't Mr. Sylvester ever tell her that during the European Dark Ages, African Empires were thriving? Serita immersed herself into the studies of Dr. Henry Clark and other African American historians writings on the African continent and cultures.

Serita soon learned that "the only thing worse than being blind is having sight, but no vision."

But emotionally, Serita had become like a turtle – she would stick her emotions out, then in an instant, when she felt emotionally challenged, she would retreat inside to a safe place. One day, while out on her morning walk, Serita met a wise man who explained that she was the captain of her ship, and that only she could take control of her feelings of inferiority. Once Serita realized that she was indeed the captain of her ship and could chart the journey, she took the steering wheel, and began to turn the ship around towards a new life. She headed towards understanding, spirituality, forgiveness, self introspection, truth and reality. The way she talked to herself began to change. Her new thoughts were of empowerment, strength and spiritual healing.

When Serita set out on her new journey, her life began to change. She was rejuvenated and she began to soar! She graduated from college as well as graduate school with honors. She received numerous awards and accommodations for her community work and was included in the "Who's Who of American Women." She was most proud of her family, and the years she spent working with disadvantaged children and families. Serita would always remember what she had been told, "What the mind can conceive it can achieve."

Four Things in Life You Can't Recover:

A STONE………..after it's thrown
THE WORD………...after it's said
THE OCCASION………...after it's missed and
THE TIME………...after it's gone!

IN HOT PURSUIT
Wanda Ng

Once upon a time, on an island in the tropics, a fifty-two year-old cleaning woman worked in an office on the second floor. It faced a park where locals enjoyed picnics while listening to live music by the sea. She paused and leaned on her broom, gazing wistfully out the balcony. "I wish I could play with a band," she envisioned. With two teenage boys in high school activities and her work, it was simple wishful thinking. Besides, the last time she played, it was at impromptu gatherings with friends, decades ago.

Every Sunday, when she worked in the office and a band was playing, her dream surfaced. Today, Hawaiian music drifted on the warm breeze coming through open doors of the lanai. The weather hardly varied, like her job for twenty years. "I'd like to live where there are different seasons." The islands had seasons: mango, papaya, and lately, hurricane season winds which brought in plenty of dirt. Housekeeping had become very boring but the money was good on this tourist-laden island.

As she bit into her backyard banana she tried to shut down that restless feeling. "After work, I'm going snorkeling." She lived in a beach town, what did she have to complain about? "I still have that old flute," she thought as she ate the lomi lomi, a fresh salmon salad made with Hawaiian salt and seaweed.

II

Once upon a time, a middle-aged woman from Sweden, a pronounced musician since her first recital at age 13, came to an island in the tropics. She pondered her move, "I wonder if I'll find anyone who I can play music with." She found a job as a high school teacher and eventually, booked an occasional music gig. She was dreaming during recess. "I want to form a community band so that musicians new to the island would have somewhere to go." She could smell the gardenia in her hair. "Maybe a principal will donate the use of a band room." After years of getting to know teachers from other schools, she met one whose principal agreed. The band room was hers, one night a week. Still, the conductor had her doubts. "What if not enough people come to fill all of the band parts required to play marches, show tunes, and Hawaiian music. It was a small island of 40,000.

III

One Sunday, during her break at the office, the cleaning lady was reading the community events section where the announcement appeared, "Take your rusty instrument from your closet and come play with the Maui Community Band on Thursday at 7:00 p.m." She tossed the paper on the desk then picked it up again, not believing her eyes. She grabbed the broom and gently swept the pile of dirt as a small feather evaded the dustpan. "Those pesky Mynah birds on the lanai!" she frowned. A Mynah bird is the size of a skinny crow but gray with a bright yellow beak. It walks like a chicken with its head leading a body that plays catch up with each step. They were fun to watch as they bickered and were hard to scare. One day she saw two of them playing with a thin plastic grocery bag. Each had a handle in its beak pulling the bag with more resistance as it completely filled up with the wind, hopping up and down with wings a flutter to stop from falling on their beaks.

She bent over to pick up the feather and dropped it above the basket, watching it float down. A quiet passionate fire was smoldering inside her. Doubt and fear was non-existent. She would be there that evening. At home, she blew on her old tarnished flute. After closing the case, she added new duct tape to its hinges. Her husband agreed to hold down the fort that evening and every evening she needed for this class.

IV

A matronly woman wearing a tight bun, sat next to her in the band room with a silver flute that had a brand-new shine. "I think I need to put on my sunglasses," the onlooker joked as she watched her buff and tactfully assemble it. "This is two years old. I just take care of it, that's all," she remarked. The dreamer clumsily assembled her dark tarnished flute and placed it on her lap, feeling unkempt. The conductor stood behind the podium and noticed the ti leaf, a Hawaiian symbol of blessing. After she welcomed the solid turnout with the excitement of a child's delight, the musicians placed their handouts on their music stands. "Shall we begin?" On the down stroke of the baton, everyone started at the same precise time, playing as though they were a flock of doves flying in unison, rising and falling in synchronization with the notes, sounds combined harmoniously in the air.

The cleaning lady tried to read the first line. By the time she thought she could catch up, they ended the song. The flute hadn't left her lap. A lost, sinking feeling of "What am I doing here?" was felt in her hot, embarrassed face. She thought she should leave but hearing the rich musical tones of tubas, clarinets, drums, saxophones, and flutes made her stay in her chair. The words "community" and "rusty" came to mind. That's what it said, so she nervously stayed. She covered the flute on her lap with her hands, waiting to hear what the conductor had to say. "Wow! I can see with all of this talent, it won't be long before our first concert." She smiled as she addressed conductors, professionals, and college graduate musicians. "I want you to know how glad I am to have you here," and her gaze extended to the end of the row where the cleaning lady sat. Watching the baton, they cued in to begin an even longer song. The tired cleaning lady loved hearing all of the instruments. Her eyes closed.

In her dream, the flute sounded unique, like a bird singing. She looked around the room to see who was playing so magically. It was coming from a baby Mynah bird on the podium. It was chubby with its first feathers but was crooning perfect tones when suddenly, down came the baton striking and breaking it into a thousand pieces of glass. She heard yelling which got louder as she awoke to hear the trumpets blaring. She recalled her music teacher in fourth grade yelling at her because she didn't practice enough. "It's my second chance," her heart had been awakened. The conductor told everyone how well they played even though a little work was needed for their first concert. As though smiling at the housekeeper, she added, "The important thing is to come back every week and we'll get there."

At the next meeting after a song, the flute player next to her, said, "You're not going to learn by leaving it on your lap." That made her smile. They read so fast, she was at a loss as to where they were but she didn't want to put her flute down either. So she chose a note here and there to play, it didn't matter which one. No one could hear her soft, rusty toot against the horns and drums. Everyone seemed quite relaxed about her presence.

For the longest time, awkwardness accompanied each practice since it took time to learn to read this new language. Many times, she was lost as they played. "Could I ever, really be part of this band?" she wondered doubtfully, as she drove, while listening to practice recordings. The conductor gave some tips while conducting, but it was pretty much left up to her to learn music notations from other members who wanted to play, not teach. She became her own teacher with the taped recordings and sheet music to piece it together. The fragrant smell from the plumeria tree came through the screened window as she learned how to breathe into the flute. Practices would last until her lips became numb or her neck sore.

Sometimes, only a few people attended and the conductor wondered what happened to all of those at the first meeting. It would take longer than she thought. An oboe player briefly joined them at the age of 12. Later, he became the youngest player to be accepted by the Honolulu Symphony. This unschooled rusty flute player was trying to blend in with some serious musicians. She had to remind herself that no one's life depended on her, just the sound of an entire band! The worse enemy was her imagination.

The conductor worked with the inconsistent attendance. She modified simpler pieces substituting *"la la la"* for the missing sections. Each practice was led with the same encouraging smile no matter how few were present. After a year, the new flute player began to see dramatic changes. Reading notes and rhythms began to fall into place. At one practice, she was the only one in the flute section. She had to play the solo and everyone would clearly hear. Exciting, but intimidating. There was only one way to go. "My dream is really coming true," she beamed inside. The other players started, and then the conductor nodded to the flute. It was her time to fly. On beat, one note at a time whistled from that old shiny flute, and the rest of the band finished. "I was part of it, really part of it, dependably so!" When she finished "Memory" from the musical Cats, she sat in a composed flute position holding back tears of joy. At another practice, she played a Hoagie Carmichael solo and the rest of the band applauded.

It was over a year before the Maui Community Band made their first appearance at Kaahumanu Shopping Mall. She wasn't nervous. All doubts were erased at practice. During the band's third-year performance, they played at Kalama Park. The conductor announced the flautist's departure to the audience. Later, she told her that she never knew anyone to learn so fast. As the night descended upon a pink Maui sunset, she headed toward her car with a sentimental thought. She and the conductor had become friends, enjoying a jazz cafe after practice. Her children had moved away to attend college. Now she could realize her biggest wish, to move where the weather was seasonal. Where her last concert was, seemed like a testimony to her journey. As she strode across the grass through a large flock of Mynah birds, farewell emotions lingered deep within. Suddenly, she was surrounded by loud flapping sounds, wings almost brushing her face. Exhilarated by the commotion, her arms stretched upwards as they flew toward the tall coconut palms. As she gazed past the shadow of her hands to the dark sky with shining bright stars, she felt she had touched one.

Two strangers brought together by a dream. At times, the rewards seemed too manini** for their efforts, but inherently they understood that to give any less would not be enough. From different countries, with extremely different skills, their dreams came true together.

*****

"To John"

*lanai-balcony

**manini-small; a juvenile fish species so named. Its glowing blue color is lost in maturity

MY LIFE'S BOUQUET
Hildy Pehrson

With arms extended, he stood in the doorway,
two crutches resting on his sides,
calling a hearty, "Welcome!"
I closed the car door, walked to him
into his encircling arms.
His hug was the kind I like best;
strong, firm, just a little bit longer than normal.

We spent some time getting reacquainted,
three months since our last visit.
"So how is your knee?" and "How was your drive?"
He managed to move around fairly well on his crutches.
I followed, touring his house.
His smile and mine went on and on.

Dinner, baked salmon,
an artistically arranged salad.
We talked and talked.
I went away a day later, promised to be back.

Each return a warm hug, the best,
with long talks and soon short walks.
Eventually, conversations became long phone calls.
Much life history exchanged, and many long embraces when together.

Now we share the mountains, sea, hills and nature's bounty
with pleasure of each other daily.
Our garden lives. We gather the blooms for each other.

MANZANAR FOR TAD
Hildy Pehrson

The wind lifts the dirt and spreads it to our eyes, mouths and hair.

We walk woodenly on the hard-packed path past the box-shaped buildings called "quarters" Everything we were allowed to bring is wrapped in bags, packs and duffels, carried on our backs and in our arms.

Others are walking quietly to other destinations, their faces stoic and rigid.

As we near the number we were assigned our burdens seem heavier than ever.

The door opens and we step inside.

The dark room is empty, much like the vacant space in our bodies and minds.

There is nothing but a small stove. It must be for cooking and heating.

Some bed-frames are shoved along one wall.

A small table and one chair wait silently in the middle of this ugly room.

The five of us will have to find a way to live in this our half of the box.

The wind and cold seeps through the boards, bringing the dirt inside.

The question "Why?" stings our hearts as the cold wind chaps our faces.

We are in our place, but it is not home.

I AM A TROPICAL BEAUTY
Reme F. Pick

My name is Cattleya Orchid. My heritage comes from South America, but I had to grow up in Los Angeles because my Aunt Alice's husband, Hector, was a merchant seaman and he escorted my mother across the ocean to lead a boring life in this city.

I lived a very sedentary life after Phillip, my owner's nephew, sliced my roots from my mother's to give to Reme. I really felt like an orphan because Reme came to see me only four times a year. She was from Pleasanton. Who ever heard of Pleasanton? Must be some honky-tonk town somewhere in America. Anyway, whenever Reme would visit her sister, she would ooh and aah when she saw how well I was growing with my roots extending upwards of the bark I was growing in.

I had been living with Aunt Alice because Reme said she could not take care of me. It seems the weather in Pleasanton was too hot in the summer and too cold during winter for orchids. What a ridiculous excuse! She just didn't want to take care of me because I am a rare and delicate specimen of an orchid. I am a Trianae specie and she had no experience in the caring of orchids. I know this because I heard the two sisters talking about me, right in front of me. Can you imagine their nerve?

Phillip was a thoughtful caretaker. He would cover me with a green protective shade when it was hot in summer and hang me inside the warm and cozy living room during the winter. I couldn't stand the music he would play on the radio though, because it made a nervous plant out of me. He would blast the radio so loud, it made me want to shout at him, but I would let my leaves quiver instead. He made sure to turn the music off when he would hear his mother's car coming in the driveway.

I am very particular about the fertilizers I consume because I have a special formula to keep my seduction and sexy flower in exotic shapes. I need ammonia and a mixture of several elements such as phosphate, magnesium, manganese, copper, and zinc. Phillip would mix these special ingredients so that my leaves would shine lustrously and give my extending tendrils strength to attach myself to the bark because, as you know by now, I am an epiphyte.

Suddenly one day, there was a buzz and excitement in Aunt Alice's house. Immediately there was going to be a wedding in her family. A granddaughter was getting married and the entire family was going to attend it in California. Ah ha, Aunt Alice thought, this time I can take the orchid with me and drop it in Pleasanton. According to my eavesdropping, I heard that the reason Reme never brought me home was because she could not take me with her on an airplane.

The moment I arrived in Pleasanton, Reme sprayed me with water. I was irritated by being in the car for seven hours and the back of my bark was drier than a desert. Reme had prepared a shady nook in the corner of her small, mosaic-tiled patio which was covered with a bamboo shade. She had a collection of geraniums, gorgeous epiphlimums that bore red and white cactus orchids, but nowhere near as dazzling as my exotic blooms. It was a pleasure for me to be welcomed by her insignificant plants and the three humming birds fighting for their territorial rights.

I knew I would be taken care of very well when two days after being in her care, Reme laid me down on a plastic stool and put the shower on for five minutes. Even the sphagnum moss and the Spanish moss hanging on my main roots sighed with utter relief for we needed the drenching after the trip.

I have become very famous because Reme showed me off to the manager of the apartments and I was pleased that they all admired my outstanding beauty and mild fragrance, but mostly that they recognized what a rare species I am. Tonight she is taking me to her writers group to show me off again.

By the way, I have forgiven Reme for neglecting me the last seven years.

MY ARMS ACHE
Pat Purvis

Here I sit in the waiting room of an infertility clinic. The décor of the room is very "Zen" to make all who wait here calm, serine and carefree. Bamboo covers the walls. There is a stone water feature gurgling on one wall. A framed fireplace flickers and crackles in the center of the opposite wall. Tall, bright red ceramic end tables sit vibrantly between the waiting chairs. Tables have blooming orchids giving off a soothing sense of color and fragrance. All the senses are touched with calm, positive waves. All this calm draws your eyes to the four windows that close off the office area. They have etched into them the egg, the fertilized egg, the blastocyst and in the final window the embryo ready for implantation on your road to a family.

I've spent my time on the internet trying to learn these terms, and afraid I'll see statistics that I don't want to know. Sometimes ignorance is bliss! As I sit in this strange world of peaceful surroundings that don't begin to take away the stress and the strain of the unknown, I think. What is this procedure like? Will it work? Where will the money for another attempt come from? No interior designer's best work can bring peace to those of us waiting in this Zen room.

I look at the other couples entering. A Chinese couple come in and registers at the desk. The lady is very petite, her black hair to her shoulders, with bangs cut perfectly straight across just above her eyes. The man is tall but seems very uncomfortable and unable to sit patiently. They were asked for $1,200 and it seemed they might not be "called" beyond the next door if they didn't write the check. Next to arrive was a tall man in shorts and a polo shirt with the very beginnings of gray at the temples. He came in alone and I wondered if he was in the wrong place, but he explained at the office window that his wife was out in the car with their son. I wondered if invetro fertilization had been necessary for that son's birth, or was this their first venture into this nerve racking world. Next through the door were two women. One went to the window and the other sat down so I concluded she must have come for moral support. But then they called her up to the window for her insurance information and I realized that baby, if they were lucky enough to get a baby, was going to have two mommies. Lastly entered the wife (I must have missed her husband going out to sit in the car with their son). She was asked for a payment of $9,000. This is pricey, this world of dividing cells that make your life worth living or break your heart into pieces that may never heal.

I wonder what stage in the process these couples are. What procedure are they having done today? The really big question on all our faces is – will this work?

One by one someone comes to the door and calls each couple in, but no one calls me. I'm not called in because there is no test for me, no results, and no answers. I'm not the one going in. My daughter is.

My husband and I have only one daughter. She is our pride and joy. She is kind, and loving and caring. She is great at organizing things just like me. She shows you how she feels if you are a disappointment to her just like her father. We've never had a sleepless night caused by her. She even married a man we love and care for nearly as much as we care for her. We count ourselves very lucky but now we share her infertility sadness and there is nothing we can do except be here and share whatever comes.

Today's itinerary was to drive 70 miles to the clinic, and wait while the embryos, grown from her eggs and collected five days ago, are placed in her perfectly ready uterus to grow into our grandchild. All the decisions that have to be made are all theirs. All the support we can give is all ours.

Even during this stressful, tense time we have our sense of humor. As our daughter was called back into the area where we all hope miracles will happen, she leaned over to me and whispered into my ear, "Mom, don't tell all the couples in the waiting room that you and Dad are here to try and get pregnant!"

Following the egg retrieval, and upon learning she had "delivered" twenty-six eggs, I showed my excitement for her with my "happy song and dance." Later, in the car, I informed her that I was going to look for a bumper sticker that read "I'm proud of my egg producing daughter!"

She was happy to be able to eat finally and her always comforting husband pulled out the goodie bag he had prepared and offered her the pick. Now we head the 70 miles home and the wait until we know the outcome. She showed us the ultrasound picture of the two little embryos sweetly nestled in. Now my turn to help begins, so I sit with her during her days of rest, trying with all my might to keep her entertained to prevent her from getting too worried, scared or bored. We talked, played games, watched TV, and sorted and organized her things since that's what we're great at.

Finally the day of the pregnancy test arrived. They went for the blood draw early in the morning and then waited. The minutes passed by so slowly. She was at work trying to stay busy. I was at home unable to concentrate on anything. The minutes turned to hours, and with every hour that passed the roller coaster ride I felt we were on was getting worse. One moment my mind was planning baby showers and baptisms and just as quickly I would fall to the lowest place with no idea how to comfort these distraught parents if the results were bad.

Finally the phone call came from our son-in-law. It was over, there is no baby! We want to be grandparents and an infertility problem stands in our way. I don't have to have regular blood draws, or ultrasounds, no MRI's, or dozens of shots and pills and special diets. But the pain of infertility is real and strong and sad. Where do we go from here?

We take that 70 mile drive to a clinic and we sit in that Zen waiting room and wait until it's our turn for that very special miracle.

MY FAMILY'S MOSAIC
Pat Purvis

Mosaic – the art of creating images with an assemblage of small pieces of colored glass, stone, or other materials.

Those words tell the definition of mosaic but it has a different meaning for me. Mosaic is the ability to touch my past and connect with my ancestors in a very special way. When I want to reach out and touch my past I visit a house on Warren Avenue where I have gone as far back as I can remember. The house was built for my great-grandmother and great-grandfather, Addie and Frank, in 1893, the same year they married. I've never known any of the owners of the house, but the house itself speaks to me with stories of my past.

The history goes back five generations from when Frank's grandparents came to America. They came through Ellis Island and then took a train to Boone County, Illinois, and brought with them special mementos from their families. Young couples leaving for America were often never able to afford to return for a visit and knew they might never see their loved ones again, so items to touch and hold were very important.

Even when these special things were broken and smashed during shipping or moving, they were never thrown away and it was customary to pass even the broken pieces on to the next generation, along with the stories of the memories that went with them.

So when my great-grandparent's house was being built, they gave a special gift to future ancestors. Around all the first-floor windows is a wide border of cement in which are laid the broken "assemblage of small pieces of colored glass" as well as broken pottery and ceramics from past generations of our family.

There are pieces of her grandmother's Sunday dishes. They were heavy ceramic dishes with tiny pink roses on them. Originally they had a silver edge but it had long been washed away. Her grandmother only used that set for Sunday dinner and when her great granddaughter was leaving for far away America, she gave her one place setting and told her to eat each Sunday dinner on those dishes to always be close to her family.

From Addie's parents, Henry and Louis, they had pieces of a set of large crockery bowls of assorted bright colors. Addie remembered them because every holiday her mother would make large batches of food in them to share with neighbors and relatives. She remembered her mother humming as she fixed cakes, and potato salad and Thanksgiving dressing in these bowls and would let her children lick them out when she had finished.

Frank's parents, Andrew and Catherine, gave them pieces of tiles that were made by Frank's grandfather in the old country. The colorful tiles decorated the fireplace, table tops, and steps and were around the doorways of their home. He sent them along with his son on his adventure to America to use in his own house someday to make it feel like home.

Addie included the pieces of her china doll head from her childhood. She had seen this beautiful dolly in a store window she walked past every day. Her love for it grew and grew and she even named it Mary Elizabeth. She would stop outside the window and talk with Mary Elizabeth about her family, how she was doing in school, even about how tough things were for her family with very little money. She prayed each night that she would get the dolly for Christmas and then would lie awake feeling so guilty that she would pray about such a thing as a doll when the family's prayers were for jobs, food, heat, clothing, and a roof over their heads. Christmas finally came and the dolly was there under the tree. She believed Santa brought Mary Elizabeth to live with her. Years later she learned that the store owner had seen her each day pouring her heart out to the doll and brought the doll, along with food and gifts for her brothers, and left it on the family's doorstep.

For his donation to the windows Frank added color and interest with his childhood collection of marbles. Frank was born several years after the end of the Civil War. By the time he was ten years old, the world economy was going well for families with more jobs, factories and work. So gifts coming from Europe would be fun items for each member of the family. A German glassblower had invented a tool in 1846 that made the sale of glass marbles to the public in Europe an economic proposition. His European family had included a bag of marbles in nearly every box sent to the states up until the time that World War I was on the horizon.

The house has had many owners since my great grandparents were gone, and lots of work has been done, but even when they had it sided they never have covered the mosaic windows that tie me to my ancestors. I think often of what will I do to pass touches of my generations to the family members to come.

TEXAS GOOD MAN
Elodia B. Resendez

"Hello there," the man on horseback said, "Come to see if anyone around knows my uncle, José Jaime. Has a place half day's ride from here." The old farmer put down his axe. "Yep, he come by ta say he wouldn't be by fer awhile. Said he was goin' ta hep fight off them meskins over San Antonio way." "Abuelo got a letter from him; it was January 1835," the rider said. He stared toward the fields, remembering that cold time, the way his grandfather gathered his grandsons in his arms, giving them the warmth they missed, as if he was trying to send his missing son comfort, wherever he might be.

"I'm Joseph. Been tryin' ta be a fine rancher neighbor, ya see. Do check his place now an' agin." The old man took a good glance at the rider, who did look like his long-gone friend, the green eyes, sitting tall in the saddle, sun-burned face, even under the wide- brimmed hat.

The rider dismounted, then stomped a leg, raising a cloud of dust as he gave it the touch of the land. He squared his shoulders, turned, got a jug from a saddlebag, opened it, and drank one gulp."*Gracías,*" he said. "Abuelo's not heard from him again. Sent me to come see about things at the place." The horse neighed, moved his head to one side, then the other, shook his tail, lifted a hoof, scuffed the ground with it, raising a storm of dust. The farmer sidled up to the horse, patting a jowl hard.

Next he gently touched the horseman's arm, thinking that would somehow help José, wherever he may be. "Your uncle sells me his livestock an' such, took up his'n guns, horse, an' joined army men who come ta sign 'im up. He told me so, sorta nervous like, ya see." Disapproval rang in his tone. "He coulda high tailed it over the Rio Grande, to his gran daddy's ranch an' fer sure, he'd still be aliving, don't ya reckon?"

"Tío joined a Texas militia. No, *Señor*, he wouldn't hide; loves his land here. Not real close to the rest of the family. A loner, my Tío was, or is." The rider's voice trailed off.

The farmer crossed his arms upon his chest. He felt a coolness, although the day was warming. "I always reckon'd he's one of them

Texans who don't like the meskin governmint tellin' 'im what ta do," he said. "I don't cares which governmint I lives under," he continued, "long as they leave me ta my bidness an' long as they leave them injuns alone too. They's happy, the wife an' I's happy, if ya know what I mean." The farmer picked up his axe and stepped backwards to the woodpile.

"*Sí*, Indians are men too. Remember, I'll be at Tío's place. Plan to stay a while." He gave the old man a piercing look. "You should know Tío José left his wife and sons, José and Joseph with my grandmother and Abuelo." "I'll be danged," the old man said, after a long pause. His faced relaxed to a soft sag; his tired eyes brighter now. "Well, glad ta know they's fine. José's a good man." The rider mounted, said "*Adíos*," and rode off.

ON THE ROAD TO VERA CRUZ
Belinda Ricklefs

We were rolling along, Smitty, Hal and I, up the eastern coast of Mexico toward Vera Cruz in Hal's old VW bug when dusk fell. We hadn't intended that. We had gotten an early start, but a side trip to check out some pre-Columbian masks made us miss the early ferry. We were tired.

"Don't drive at night," people told us. "There are black cows wandering unfenced in that area, and you can't see them at night."

We weighed the choices: invisible black cows vs. doubtful lodging in the one tiny port town we could reach before dark. We took some Benzedrine and headed north.

It was spring of 1963, and this was the last leg of a month-long holiday the three of us were taking on the pretext of hunting down pre-Columbian artifacts in Mexico and Guatemala. Hal was my boyfriend— and we were breaking up. No hard feelings, just no more juice. We both wanted an adventure. Smitty, Hal's buddy from Korean war days, was along because he actually knew a lot about pre-Columbian artifacts. He also was great company. The three of us had fun together, and Smitty communicated for all of us in Spanish. Hal, with a mother from El Salvador and a father from England, understood Spanish like a native but hated to speak it. I didn't want to speak it either. I didn't want to sound stupid limping along with my ten words of third-grade Spanish. Smitty loved talking to people and picked up the language in a whiz.

The night turned dark: no moon, and only a few stars shining through the cloud cover. The road ran straight, raised about four feet above the fields, a black line on a black background. We saw the cow's eyes gleaming in the headlights twenty feet away. Hal swerved, and we ploughed over the left side of the road rolling the car. We didn't hit the cow. The next I knew, I was lying barefoot on my back in a field.

"Hal?" I said. "Smitty?"

Smitty's voice came out of the dark, "Are you OK?"

"I think so. I just need to lie here a minute." The earth felt good under me, solid and reassuring. "Are you OK?"

"Yeah, I'm fine," Smitty said. He had been dozing in the back, curled up on our stuff. We had removed the back seat and made a nest of all our clothes and sleeping bags. I turned my head to look at the car. It was upside down with two broken windows. I almost remembered squeezing myself through a window, driven by a primal need to get the hell out. The thought distantly crossed my mind that I might have gouged my back on the broken glass.

"Hal." I said, "Where's Hal? Is he OK?"

"I'm fine," Hal's voice said out of the darkness. Then their faces appeared, looking down at me with worried expressions. They squatted down next to me. "Can you get up? "

"I guess so," I said, but I didn't. Vertical seemed like a difficult concept. I wondered if I was in what people call a state of shock.

"Please," Hal said, "try."

What's the rush, I thought. Guys. They always need instant action. I'm fine. Why not rest here a bit longer and relax? Or is this like freezing? You think you're warm and comfy when actually you're about to die. They looked so worried I almost laughed. But their hands were reaching out so I reached back, grabbed hold and sat up.

"Look," I said pointing at my feet, "no shoes. I must have jumped right out of them, just like they say happens in car crashes. Your body jumps out of its shoes." Saying words out loud made me feel more real. I walked around a little to see if I could and found my shoes five feet away. Everything else had stayed inside the car.

The road was not well traveled, but ten minutes later, we saw headlights coming toward us from Vera Cruz. It was a bus, and it stopped. Men tumbled out and ran down to us with much shouting.

"What happened? Are you OK? Oh yes, black cows, dangerous. Bandits too."

A bunch of them rocked the VW until it was right side up. The engine ran, but we had two flat tires. After lengthy animated discussion, they came up with a plan. One of the men, a fellow named Panchito, was to stay with Hal and me to protect us from bandits. Smitty would jump on the bus with the other men and the two flat tires. They would get the tires patched in the little port town we had passed 20 miles before. Then Panchito's brother, who lived in the town, would drive Smitty and the tires back, and we would follow the two brothers back to the town. There would be a room available at the hotel, and the adventure would come to a happy conclusion.

The bus drove off with all its bustle, carrying Smitty with it. The night seemed suddenly desolate and huge. We climbed into the car to wait. Hal gazed out at the blackness, hands resting on the wheel. Panchito, machete drawn, occupied the passenger's seat, and I perched on our stuff in the back.

"What happened?" Hal asked.

"What do you mean?"

"Don't kid around. What happened? Why are we in this field? Where's Smitty?"

"Well," I said warily, "There was a cow in the road, and you swerved to miss it, and we rolled over. Then these guys stopped to help us. Smitty's getting the tires fixed. He'll be back soon."

"Oh," Hal said. Panchito fiddled with the glove compartment. Then he turned around to experimentally fiddle with my bare knee showing under the hem of my skirt. Close quarters in a VW bug. I casually shifted my knee away from his hand.

Hal turned to look at me. "What happened?" he asked. "What are we doing here? Who's the guy with the machete? Where's Smitty?"

"We had an accident," I said. "This is Panchito. He's protecting us from bandits. Smitty will be back soon. He's getting the tires fixed." Panchito turned the machete over a few times in his hand.

"Oh," Hal said.

And so it went for the next hour and a half. Every minute or so, Hal would ask what had happened and I would tell him. Panchito would experiment with my knee and admire his machete, and I would pull down my skirt. About an hour in, Panchito asked to look at Hal's watch, a handsome gold one. Hal gave it to him, and he put it on. I saw it happen with clear, sharp precision as if in slow motion.

"Hal," I managed.

"What?"

"Your watch…" My voice faded away.

I imagined Panchito thinking the watch was a nice tip. I imagined Hal thinking that it was a fair exchange for protecting us from bandits. I imagined Panchito murdering us. I imagined Panchito slipping out of the car, signaling his bandit friends to swoop down and murder us. My throat closed up. What am I doing, I thought, making up scary stories. I couldn't do anything if someone did try to murder me. I can't even rescue Hal's watch.

Hal looked at me in the rearview mirror. "What happened?" he asked. "Where's Smitty? Who's the guy with the machete?"

It seemed an eternity before we heard the car that brought Smitty and the tires back. We got the Bug rolling, following Panchito and his brother very slowly back to the port town. Panchito's brother had even found a place off the street to park the car which was pretty banged up. "Better not let the cops see it," he said. "They'll give you a ticket for driving a wrecked car."

About 11:00 that night, we found a tiny hotel, but since we weren't sleepy yet, we explored the port. It was still buzzing with activity. We ate fresh papayas, the best I've ever had, and chatted with an American writer who was living there for a few months while he worked on a play. We found a doctor. Both Hal and I had gashes on our backs from climbing through broken glass. I hadn't felt mine until he put antiseptic on them. It turned out that Hal also had a concussion.

"I'm calling an ambulance to take you to Vera Cruz tomorrow," the doctor told him, "And for God's sake, go lie down and stop walking around."

The ambulance arrived the next morning. It was a small white van with two guys up front, both wearing caps that said "Sherwin Williams Paint Covers the Earth." They loaded Hal onto a cot in the back of the van. I got in too before they could protest. Smitty stayed behind to deal with the car.

We drove very slowly to Vera Cruz, maybe 20 miles an hour so as to not aggravate Hal's concussion. Mariachi music blared from the radio the whole time. I rode perched on a stool, craning my neck to peer out the windshield. When we came to the outskirts of Vera Cruz our paramedics slowed down even more, veering the van close to the sidewalk to ogle and joke with groups of pretty girls.

The hospital in Vera Cruz looked like a small hotel with a lovely tiled inner courtyard, complete with fountain, and rooms around the edge. I did see one cockroach in the bathroom. I didn't tell Hal. I helped him get set in his room, but the staff wouldn't let me stay. Being the girlfriend did not give me visiting privileges. Hal eventually persuaded them that I was his second cousin, and then they let me visit from 2:00 to 3:00 each afternoon. He asked again and again for the story of what had happened. I filled in details until he had them memorized. When he asked where his watch was, I told him he had given it to Panchito, the machete guy. For Hal, that was just one more incomprehensible detail in an unreal event. He hadn't been there.

I hung around Vera Cruz for a couple of days, sightseeing on foot and by streetcar, taking every line to the end and back. I ate in two small restaurants and bought magazines for Hal. It seemed like a wind-up toy city: every day the same bells, the same streetcars in their circuits, the same people on the same errands. My favorite scene was the after dinner ritual in the plaza. Young women walked counter clockwise on the inside track of the wide sidewalk, laughing with each other and flirting with the young men who walked clockwise on the outside track. The men posed and joked when they caught a girl's eye. I watched from the benches on the sidelines along with the chaperones. Popcorn and ice cream vendors held down the corners.

Smitty arrived the day I had to take a bus to Mexico City to catch my flight home. Hal stayed two more days in the hospital and another week in Mexico while he and Smitty dealt with the car. It was against the law to drive it, there were no parts to fix it, and he had to get special papers to leave the country without it. The two of them took the train back to the States.

That fall I went to Europe and ended up staying three years. Hal went to Southeast Asia to work and married a woman from Vietnam. We have seen each other from time to time over the years. We always have lunch at a Mexican restaurant. We talk about kids and projects, the food and the weather. At some point, he always asks me what happened that night on the road to Vera Cruz.

AGE STRONG! LIVE LONG!
Pat Roper

From the Great Depression to a time of plenty characterizes our lives. The experiences of the former allow us to fully appreciate the later. What of the many years in between? There is growing up through childhood, becoming educated and learning the skills to make a living. The road has had many ups and downs, more ups than downs. God always gives us a way if we are willing to trust in Him, we have learned to trust in the goodness of God. To age strong you must work and pray as hard as you can.

Our choice of spouse is a critical decision as it shapes our life journey in every way. You can no longer be first, you learn that you have to put your spouse first as you share the good and the bad times. To age strong you must love unconditionally.

Once the children arrive you have to share more and more, spreading yourself thinner and thinner. The conflicts in parenting can test a marriage and put husband and wife at odds with one another. You learn to show a united front to your children and if you do disagree, do so in private…to age strong, you must stay strong together.

Happiness comes from within…we learned early on that people and possessions cannot make us happy. There are only happenings that may enrich our lives but our true happiness comes from within as we live our lives in accordance with our beliefs. To age strong you need a strong faith foundation and a willingness to set self interests aside for the good of one's marriage and family.

As marriage moves from passionate love to a phase of deep abiding love it is important to look forward and never look back. To age strong we need to accept one another as we are today with love, gentleness, kindness and a sense of humor.

There is only one you, so don't try to be someone you are not. It helps to learn from one another, but don't let another take over the essence of who you are. To age strong you must continually grow and discover more about whom you are…your authentic self.

The retirement from our labors should motivate us to help others and share our acquired skills, knowledge and even wisdom. To age strong we must continue to learn, to participate in life and to share our gifts.

God tells us to share what we have. There will always be heartbreak, but God will be with us to the end of our journey. Enjoy the gifts He has given. The golden years become a bouquet of memories…it is never too late to enlarge your bouquet with grandchildren, great grandchildren and newfound friends. To age strong you must stay open to new people, new ideas and new experiences…without losing your authentic self.

May God grant us the grace to age strong, just as He gave us the gift to live long!

SACRED SPACE
Irene Sardanis

I entered the inner sanctum
My office
smooth black leather couch
where my giant ego
had been crushed
repeatedly
by human pain and sorrow
It took a lifetime
to learn to listen
to just shut up
Dr. know–it–all

Now I know I did not know
I bore witness to
countless outrage
At days end I was on my knees
alone
humbled
at being chosen
to do a job
I wish
I had learned
to do better

SINGING
Irene Sardanis

When we were children, my sister and I were forced to perform in front of relatives. They always laughed at our efforts to sing. After my father left us, our family was poor so could not afford a television. There wasn't anything else. We were the entertainment.

My older sister sang first. She had a strong beautiful voice, and was always a hard act to follow. My mother would push my scrawny nine-year-old body in front of the room full of aunts, uncles and cousins and say to me, "You sing good now." I did not want to sing. I felt fear and terror that I would not do well, that my mother would punish me for not making her proud. I'd get that certain look from her, together with a pinch on my arm that made me tremble inside if I did not perform to her high standard. I held my hands together as I sang, "You Are My Sunshine." After I sang, I got a pat on my behind. I passed the test again

Through the years I learned to love jazz so that as an adult when I read about a Jazz Camp for all levels of experience, I sent in my money and registered to attend. I signed up for morning jazz dance, and jazz vocals in the afternoon. My teacher, Madeline Eastman, performed in jazz clubs around the San Francisco area. She stood in front of the class, dressed in shorts, tank top and sandals.

The class was full, about twenty men and women. The first woman who volunteered to sing sang like an angel. She looked at all of us boldly in the eyes and belted out that song like she owned it. She was confident, stood tall and proud, just what I didn't have at all I was stunned, speechless at the quality of her voice. I perspired, shrank into my seat.

I had made a huge mistake, was in over my head, in the wrong place and the wrong time, about to be booted out as soon as anyone heard me squeak out my song. The rest of the class was a blur. The same fear and terror I felt as a child, I experienced again. I wanted to sneak out of camp, hoping no one would take notice. When the class was over, I walked up to my vocal teacher.

"Miss Eastman," I blustered, starting to cry.

"What's wrong?" she asked.

"I think I've made a terrible mistake," I said. "I thought I could take this jazz vocal class with you, but I can't. Everyone here is more advanced than me. I think I better go back home." I turned to leave, but she stopped me and took my hands firmly in hers and looked at me directly.

"Do you know the song you want to sing?" she asked.

"There will Never be Another You," I whispered, "a Chet Baker standard."

"Okay. Here's what I want you to do," she said, as though she were now giving me the secret ingredients to a special cake recipe. "I want you to talk with the faculty here, like Denise Perrier, Mark Levine, jazz pianist. Ask them for the key you're going to sing in and practice the piece all week. If you can't sing it in the class by Friday, I'll send you home."

I was determined to do everything she suggested. I was excited and challenged to do my very best for this teacher who was taking me under her wing.

The next morning in Denise Perrier's class, I clung to the piano as I sang, holding onto it as though it were a life raft, my voice tight with tension. She looked at me and smiled.

"Is that the way you gonna deliver that song to us, darlin'?" she asked in her honey-coated voice. "Why don't you let go of the piano, stand tall and look at all of us, okay? We ain't gonna bite you. We want to hear what you got to say." This was a classy singer, we called The Diva. She asked me first to speak the words to the song as though it were a poem, then sing it. It worked. I felt more relaxed and more connected to the song, the accompanist and the class audience.

Each day that week I asked teachers and students to help me with the song, to listen to me sing it, to correct my posture, my presentation, my delivery of the piece. I sang it in class, with and without backup musicians. Every which way I sang that song at the camp walking to class, to the trees, around camp, to the kitchen staff, to the cats and dogs, the birds, to anyone willing to listen. Morning, noon and night I sang that song. In my sleep, I sang the song.

Originally, the plan was to sing in Ms. Eastman's class at the end of the week. The only slot available, the staff said, was for me to sing in the amphitheater, where all students perform their piece at the end of the week as a certificate of graduation. I had prepared. Still anxious, I hardly slept the night before. Friday I felt ready to sing my song. I dressed for the occasion, put on make-up and even borrowed a skirt and earrings from a fellow camper. It was time, show time.

They were all there, fellow Jazz Campers that last evening as I approached the amphitheater to sing. There were only three steps to reach the stage but it felt as though I were climbing Mount Everest. Where I was forced to perform as a child, now I wanted to sing. Now I could sing my own song. I looked into the audience of 200 Jazz Campers, all strangers when I arrived the week before, now a loving family.

Where I once felt pressured to sing, now with a full heart I wanted to sing, I stood there and opened my arms and sang "There Will Never Be Another You."

In the front row I saw my teacher. She was wiping tears from her eyes.

WHAT IF
Claude Shaver

The word "if" has been called the BIGGEST word in the English language. Combined with the word "what", it opens the door to infinite speculation and becomes the Yellow Brick Road into the vast realm of the Twilight Zone.

What if ...

General Washington had surrendered to Lord Cornwallis at Yorktown in 1781?

General Grant had surrendered to General Lee at Appomattox in 1865?

America had not entered World War One and turned the tide of battle in 1917?

Hitler and the Nazis had remained a minor political party and never gained power?

The German Air Force had dropped the first atomic bomb?

President Kennedy had survived his assassin's bullets in 1963?

The Soviet Union had not collapsed but had gotten more powerful?

The Cold War had heated up and reached the boiling point while teetering on the brink of war?

The Nuclear Clock had finally struck Twelve?

What if...

ARMAGEDDON'S LEGACY

>Oh Intelligent MAN
>
>Look what you've wrought
>
>Evolution of life
>
>Has been for naught
>
>Your fiery holocaust
>
>Has blown it away
>
>Apocalypse foretold
>
>Has dominion this day

If, a curious little word, indeed.

AUTUMN GLORY
Claude Shaver

A dark formation filled with raucous calling wings beneath gray clouds
And spirals of chimney smoke dot the sky
Surrounding woodlands are ablaze with colors from an artist's palette
And there's sharpness in the air
Harvested fields have given up their bounty
A busy squirrel scampers about
Twitching ears testing the air
A gray rabbit noses around amidst the flash of darting finches
Seeking a winged repast
A strutting jay atop his leafy perch squawks his annoyance at my presence below
A wary doe creeps quietly through gathering shadows
Her young follow
Drawing my attention to the waning light
Raising my collar to the growing chill
I start back along the way I came
Taking my leave from a late autumn scene

AT THE TABLE
Tonia Stanley

My sister and I used to visit my grandmother. We would sit at her dining room table and would admire the flowers in the vase, the butter in the butter dish, the fruit arrangement in the fruit bowl. There was always soup cooking on the stove.

Before we ate she would send us to the bathroom to wash our hands and dry them on lacy- edged towels that she had crocheted.

Our grandmother was a woman before her times and a naturalist. In her cupboard there were cloves for a toothache, dry mustard for a stomachache, salt for brushing your teeth, baking soda for deodorant, Crisco lard for greasing our legs and arms. She made her own soap, and she boiled her clothes on the stove.

Mary Elizabeth was born in 1891 in Pennsylvania. She was reared in a Quaker home. My grandmother was of mixed African-American and Native-American background. She stated her grandmother was kidnapped when she was eight years old, and her grandfather, a tribal leader, was killed in a conflict when the U.S. government tried to uproot and seize Native American land. Her mother died when she was very young and her father raised her for a few years, but eventually left for Ohio to seek better opportunities. He sent her to live with her older brothers and sisters who lived in a Native-American household in Virginia. She remained there until meeting her husband, Peter, a black man who had fled the South because of family problems and the oppressive racism and threats present in the Post Civil War South.

Ironically, although her family didn't celebrate Thanksgiving, they knew that Columbus didn't discover America. She was equally proud of her African-American heritage and loved her darker skin. Back then many Native Americans had darker hues because they had not been killed or often forced to assimilate with Europeans. Her brother Frederick was a member of the first graduating class of the newly founded black college, Hampton. He served in the Union Army during the Civil War.

In Norfolk ,Virginia, she met my grandfather, who was a cook and porter on the railroads. His job was one of the few positions that was organized and afforded a black man an opportunity to work and earn a secure employment. Led by the great Civil Rights leader, A. Philip Randolph, The Brotherhood of Sleeping Car Porters was the first labor organization led by African-Americans to receive a charter in the American Federation of Labor.

When Elizabeth moved to New York City to be with her husband, she joined his church, Walker Memorial Baptist Church. She remained a member until health and old age slowed her down sixty years later. She made her transition to God when she was ninety-one years old. She was a card-carrying member of the Marcus Garvey Movement, founded by the Jamaican who came to America and started the Back-to-Africa movement. It was the first huge grassroots movement, national and international, that tried to unite all People of African descent into a political and economical force. The organization encouraged African people to be self reliant, to start and support community-based businesses. Its motto was, "Africa for Africans." At that time all of Africa, with the exception of Ethiopia, was controlled by European colonial forces. Marcus Garvey wanted to raise the plight of his people, raise the conscious and self esteem and freedom from racism and exploitation of African people, in Africa, the Caribbean, the United States and Latin America. Garvey and his organization wished to restore and acknowledge the neglected contributions and huge contributions of African people to history, culture and economical wealth of the West.

Each time we visited my grandmother she would send us around the corner for the *Amsterdam News*, the leading black newspaper in Harlem. She would have us sit at the dining room table and read to her. She would say "now let's see what black people are doing."

We learned from that paper about the black-owned bank at 125th Street in Harlem. We talked about Adam Clayton Powell. With her we learned about the accomplishment of black people. Our grandmother was very proud to be a black woman. She would extend her arm toward us, and with her finger on her other hand she would rub the skin on her arm and say "this is 100% pure black." In those times, and even today, many African-Americans were ashamed of their dark skin, or not having European physical features. She was a woman ahead of her time.

At my grandmother's table she imparted to us her sense of right and of equality. She taught us moderation in dress, speech and deportment, no doubt learned from her Quaker upbringing.

My grandmother was a consummate seamstress. She would make patterns from looking at fashions in newspapers; she would produce the most beautiful clothes. She was also one of the best dressed ladies in town. Grandma also loved to flee with her children from the hot crowded city every summer to vacation in Syracuse, New York, while her husband would be out of town, working on the railroads. There the air was cleaner, and the grass was greener. She knew people there. She would attend the racetracks and loved to bet on the horses.

As I think back, I received a wonderful education at my grandmother's table.

IN MIAMI WHEN I TOOK A WALK
Joanne Sultar

I
"Don't get lost," my mother would say
Meaning: Come back soon.
Meanng: Don't dawdle.
Meaning: Don't examine every flower.

Meaning: Don't engage in long conversations.
Meaning: This is My Time.
You belong to me.

Meaning: Please, don't get lost.

II

She
said
You are
wasting time.
Everytime I went
to dance with my muse – to fly home -
Every time I slowed inward to dream
she
said
Come back.
Do something
I can understand.

MAP OF MIAMI
Joanne Sultar

The Prompt: There was a straw basket completely filled with maps. Close your eyes – reach in - pick one.

A map! Miami! I picked out Miami! - out of the hat – out of the bag. Dade County, Miami Beach – North Miami Beach. Can I take it home? Can I paste it in my book? Can I crawl into it and will she be there like she was – standing there – waiting for me outdoors, swollen and puffed with waiting as my shuttle pulls through the gate and I am chauffeured to her nervous and exuberant expectancy and the spell that she once wove so fine and tight it lasts and lasts all through these so-called adulthood years.

Will she be there putting melmac dishes on a plastic cloth on a dining room table that someone else chose years ago before she was the renter? Proudly bringing out what she has prepared just for me - what she has prepared in the weeks prior to my visit and kept frozen in a small freezer in a tiny kitchen, what she has prepared that is like easy morphine as I sink out of my world into hers: satisfied eating, dutiful daughter, it's delicious, yes, it's delicious – and it is.

Will she be there - standing there, sitting there, waiting for me, calling to me, talking on the phone, setting the table, clearing the table, getting ready to leave, getting ready to go downstairs and why must I always carry such a big bag? What do I need to carry with me all the time? It makes no sense. It troubles her. She wants me to leave it behind, but it's my bag.

THE PAYROLL
Joanne Sultar

My mother's hair is thinner now. When we wash it, it springs into short white-gray curls with some darker areas in the back. I towel dry it and put some conditioner on. She is adorable in these moments - clean, innocent – open and fresh.

After her shower, I help dry her legs in the back where it's harder for her to reach. I find folds, creases, designs and textures that make me think of tree trunks - of a strong and ancient tree - each line so many stories. All the walking in a life – shopping to save pennies, crisp autumn morning walks to the train to work.

Once in a while on a school holiday, I'd go with her – an adventure that held wonder and magic - an actual train with a conductor taking tickets and calling out stations, slowly rolling out of the city to another world with private homes and much more green. Mr. or Mrs. Martin picked us up at the Scarsdale station and drove us to their home. The office of the construction company was downstairs.

She was so pleased going to work – she just went one day a week, and the rest she did in her home-office right there in the bedroom. The weekly payroll. The phone had a speaker, so as Mr. Martin read off the hours worked for each of the men she was able to enter the figures on large ledger sheets. I used to know the men's names by heart. She made up the pay envelopes – wrote each man's name and hours on them. By the time I was nine or ten, I helped regularly, using the adding machine with speed and skill. It felt like a toy or a competitive sport – how fast could I go without making an error? She was proud of me. She was proud of herself.

She loved bookkeeping – this small world so totally contained and easily controlled – each week balancing the ledgers – adding columns this way and that – getting totals to match total. She was satisfied – happy.

Now, I come to see her. She is waiting and focused on the tasks I need to do for her. She is sometimes confused – disoriented – slowing down – the hard edges have softened. There are bills to pay and mail to sort, but what she says is, "We have to do the payroll."

UNCLE MEYER'S REQUEST
Joanne Sultar

I was in my early or mid teens when Uncle Meyer approached me in a more serious manner; perhaps it was the first time he wasn't just joking around. We were standing in the small living room of 5-G – our apartment in the Bronx. I had never seen him look so troubled. He was upset about the son or daughter of someone close to him who had left their family and moved out to California. He told me this as if it were a tragedy – a betrayal he could not understand. He explained how family needed to stay close by - how much a heartache it is when a child goes far away.

He stood facing me, eye-to-eye, and said, "I want you to promise me you'll never do that – you'll never go so far away. Promise me that. I want you to make that promise."

My Uncle Meyer, my father's sister's husband, was one of the few men in our lives who seemed to embody success. He had a commanding presence, an ease and bravado - a confident businessman with an air of prosperity – a home on Long Island – an easy joker – always on. He was the only one who visited us who wanted a shot of whiskey from the small, usually neglected collection of bottles in the foyer closet where we hung our coats.

Uncle Meyer and I had a special connection; I was born on this birthday – his birthday niece. We often seemed in sync – an understood and understated kind of twinkle-in-the-eye. When I was little he was playful with me – bounced me on his knee, lollapaloozas on my belly - all with words I don't remember except for his announcement of that word, lollapalooza. A noisy bit of lip action that tickled – more of a game than a kiss. I don't remember being delighted by this; it may have been more fun for him than for me. Being lifted and lollapaloozed was perhaps just another surrender to the environment. Yet these occasions stand out as times I mattered to someone in a fun way – a wilder way – a lighter way than usual.

And then, years later, there he was; so very serious and asking for this promise to never move far from home and family.

Standing there I couldn't even imagine a life of my own choosing; I'd never thought about going anywhere at all – separating like that, and yet when I said "OK" or "I promise." Somehow, I knew I was lying. Not that I knew I would leave, but that I had no idea of how to even think about that possibility. I also knew it was the only response I was capable of giving.

THE CZARINA SLEEPS IN
Mei Sun Li

The Czarina sleeps in as
Servant girls glide along corridors,
Brocade vestments draped heavily over plump farm girl arms.
And the morning of this Sunday halts not at all
As clock hands move the silence along.

Two satyrs frolic, watching
As she sleeps - blessedly,
Stirring in a dream of love and the golden light
That showers the mountain valleys.

Not here but there,
Metal strikes metal and then the stone, the dull clang muffled,
Repeatedly.
Horses hooves kick, fear bludgeoning the air,
And trample
The weary soldier who prays for death
A sweet apple tucked in his pocket.

And the Czarina sleeps without foolishness,
Golden ringlets a tease on her silken pillow.

ONCE UPON A TIME
Mei Sun Li

Once upon a time, I thought all things were possible. I was very young.

I thought that I could dance – gracefully, beautifully. I could project magnificence from a theater stage. Kicking up my heels would not only be an exhilarating event – and a dependably do-able one – but the tour jete leaps, the curve of my slim arms bent into the elongated parentheses would send reverberations of great joy and awe not only into the hearts of my audiences but, especially and particularly, into my own drumming, happy one.

Once upon a time, I believed that with practice and courage, I could sing. That each embellished tone that emanated from the cavities of the whole musculature system of my oral being would soar into the heavens and there would be joy. The joy would radiate. It would bloom. And I would be so very happy.

Once upon a time, I believed that quarrels would end and that forgiveness and kindness would reign on this earth everywhere and not only in the fairy tales of my childhood.

I once believed that I could be fearless, that fearfulness was just a crippling symptom of youth, of inexperience, and would be outgrown. Just as the bright red and sting of a scraped knee would heal overnight, so would the tremor of worry, the loneliness and the dreadful not knowing, and the inability to grasp more of what was possible at each moment's juncture – all that would be mended, cured, resolved. I would finally hold this very special book of wondrous knowledge clasped tightly to my chest to be savored forever.

I once believed that I would relish my mother's laugh on a long continuum of time. That mom would stumble again and again into some bramble bushes on the craggy Lake Tahoe hike we took when she was already into her seventies, my age now, and just wave her slim legs with their JC Penney knee hi's into the air in a fit of risqué giggles, her baby blue sweater and jaunty neck scarf sealed into my memory.

I once believed that no harm would ever come to anyone I loved so dearly. That like the song, the Rockies would tumble, Gibraltar would crumble before danger would look me in the eye. I believed that we would be safe, embraced by the forces that decreed that nothing bad happened to good people. So I would be good. I would make my bed, be kind to strangers, brush my hair a hundred strokes a day and yet reject vanity. I would understand that the music of the firmaments was the only proof I needed to believe that God was generous and loving.

What a belly laugh. I am the fool. Not alone in my foolishness. Not alone in the quagmire that dictates that scraped knees heal only in the world of youthful innocence.

As I slept so lusciously secure in my mother's womb, the third eye watching the soft pink knobs of my early being turn and evolve into translucent limbs, I wonder, did the single, dual, quadruple cells of my brain have a wayward way of knowing that the soft warmth and protection of that small, contained world would erupt cruelly, and the fissures would define a rough, cold cruelty that would not end until the next ending? I can hear the beat of my mother's heart and I too know her own innocence, her trust that all would be well. Thump – thump, thump-thump. The old world of Tienjin, China, her home, the soft sliding doors leading to the gardens, the land of her girlhood, calling and drifting so far away.

I owned a doll once. Yes, I remember only one single doll and not the countless mounds of dolls and stuffed animals of every persuasion which grace the corners of my sweet grandchildren's beds. This doll, perhaps a foot tall, costumed in a simple outfit of a turquoise green hue, was literally two faced, asleep, long lashes lying on its cheeks, or wide-eyed awake. One just simply turned the head about. The act of manually turning its head into its own cap seemed odd to me even then, its own act of cruelty. One could say, if a level of distaste were to be owned up to, the doll's head could be wrenched round and round from one world to the other.

Playing with that doll was less an act of playful parenting and solace than a reflection of continual curiosity. Death and life, death and life, round and round.

Today the earth is sweet, the sun warm. I've planted tomatoes. I haven't planted tomatoes in 35 years. The deer may win out or the squirrels but today there is hope that the warm sun will illuminate the genetic system of those leafy stems. The aroma of those sturdy rich green stems and leaves fill my nostrils, and the small confines of this weed tufted patch of yard are a momentary altar to well being. The planet spins as the Hubble telescope up there, so far away up there above us, sucks in the beauty of the bigger universe which is really just another pinprick in a larger fabric. Glorious high tech Hubble space photos will soon grace a million gift shop windows. I hanker after them.

NO HARM DONE - PART 1
Mary Tate

The sun, loath to set, lingered on into the soft summer night, leaving a finger of rose in its wake. The lazy afternoon had matured into a perfect evening. Southern summer nights are always warm and friendly and still, except for the sound of crickets and bullfrogs or an occasional soft breeze that steals by on silent feet and gently rustles the leaves.

The old faded blue Chevrolet looked quite out of place moving through the exclusive section. Only the very elite lived in the beautiful homes perched high on the hills in Clarendon Heights. The car slackened its speed as it came to two stone pillars with "Dumont" on a bronze plaque imbedded in them. The car continued up the driveway and around to the back of the house. The patio had been roped off and was illuminated with Japanese lanterns inside of which were multicolored bulbs. The Chevrolet maneuvered its way to the far side and parked. A man stepped from the car and maneuvered his way though the tables and chairs arranged on the patio. The man was perhaps six feet tall with very brown skin, straight shoulders, and a slight bulge about his middle. His face was craggy. His pleasant smile revealed large white teeth with a small gap in the center. His hair was salt and pepper, wavy and cut close to his head. He entered the side door that led to the kitchen and gave a pleasant greeting to the maids who bustled about preparing hors d'oeves. The younger maid cast an admiring glance. The older maid jabbed her and said quietly, "You can forget that. He is much married with four children. Don't waste your time." The man made several trips to his car carrying ice buckets and bartender's tools. Before closing the door of the car for the last time he reached back inside and took out the stiff starched white jacket with blue collar and lapels and the single gold button at the middle.

Moses Williams was quite proud of his bartender's jacket, and as men do, secretly reveled in the thought that it was quite becoming. He had always been meticulous about his appearance. Now, newly starched and shined, he looked much younger than his fifty-six years.

A woman swept into the kitchen. She spoke pleasantly. "Good evening, Moses. I see you arrived early. Well, that's fine. There are still a million things to be done before the guests arrive."

"Good evening, Miss Helen. Sho is a nice night for a pahty. Decided to come early cause I figured you might need a little extra hep." His voice was low and pleasant. "The first thing you can do is set up the bar. Everything is waiting for you on the back porch." She adjusted the tie to her negligee, brushed the long hair up from her neck, and took a slow drag from the cigarette that she held between two long slim fingers that tapered into painted red nails.

"Saw your picture in the paper the other day, Miz Helen. That was some fish you and Mr. John caught." The woman stubbed out her cigarette in the nearby ashtray before answering. "Oh, he gave us a hell of a lot of trouble before we landed him. Moses, you'd better fix me a cocktail to welcome my coming of age. Ever since he got that damn new yacht, Dumont has been going out every Sunday. Never could see what he got out of the sport anyway. All I ever got was a few bruises, broken nails and a decent tan, which I can get in my own back yard." She took the cocktail that was being held out to her. "Helen. Helen," the impatient voice of Mr. Dumont came from the interior of the house. "Oh hell, what does he want now," she said under her breath and left the kitchen. Moses looked after her. "Sho is a fine figure of a woman. Tall and all that red hair hangin' down her back. No wonder Mr. John is so jealous of her. Got a right to be. Even if he is old enough to be her paw. Thirty some odd years ago when Dumont had come to work in the Dumont shipyards, his name was John Lee Jones. He happened to meet the boss's daughter. She was a very homely and shy girl. John Lee saw his opportunity. He courted Clara Sue and proposed marriage. Hoping for an heir, old man Dumont consented to the marriage with the stipulation that John Lee take the Dumont family name. They were wed. After five years of marriage, Clara Sue died in childbirth. The child survived only a few days. Dumont had been moving John Lee up steadily in the company. When the old man died seven years later John Lee took over the company. He turned out to be a shrewd businessman and over the years had become the wealthiest and most prominent businessman in the city. After an appropriate mourning period, Mr. Dumont took a trip up north and returned with Helen as his bride. Everyone had been quite surprised at first, but she was JL's wife. So the women instantly welcomed her, instinctively sensing, as women do, that it would be better to have this woman as an ally.

Moses mused as he went about his work. "Yesir, it was mighty good of Mr. John to let me work this party. Probably Ms. Helen's doing though. Thinks nobody kin mix a martini like I can. Beautiful night like this and that wife of mine didn't want me to come. Said she had a funny feeling. Don't know what she thought could happen here. That Lela worries about me all the time. Spec I'll call her later on and let her know everything's alright. The money from this job ought to be just enough to finish out that last payment on Lela's surprise," he smiled to himself. Mr. John rules us at the shipyard but Ms. Helen sure rules him at home. She's a mighty nice woman though. Can't seem to understand the southern ways but she's alright. Sometimes she drinks too much and gets real affectionate like the time at the Frasier's beach house on Dauphin Island. Mr. Dumont really got mad at her that night. Sho was funny though. Her insistin' on kissing every man in the room and Mr. John cursing and trotting behind her. Thought he was going to haul off and knock the stuffing out of one of those men but he didn't have the nerve I guess.

A little before nine, Mr. John and Ms. Helen came into the kitchen for a final check. Mr. John wore a brown suit, bow tie and brown and white wingtip shoes. His hair was thinning and he combed the strands over to cover the bald spot. His glasses sat high on his nose, which accentuated his receding chin. Miz. Helen appeared several moments after Mr. Dumont. Her auburn hair was parted in the middle with undulating waves framing her face and cascading down to creamy white shoulders. Her sea green dress accentuated her ample breasts and hips. The bodice was fitted and as she floated around the kitchen her tea-length skirt flared, revealing shapely ankles and feet enclosed in green matching sandals with four-inch heels. Her ears were adorned with emerald drop earrings that complemented her green eyes. On her left arm, she wore an emerald tennis bracelet and on her ring finger she wore a huge emerald encrusted with diamonds.

"Moses, did you bring them?" Mr. Dumont inquired.

"Oh yessir. I got them right here. Fresh baked just before I came."

Moses opened a box that revealed dozens of golden brown biscuits about the size of bottle caps – each one spread with a dab of country butter with a bit of ham or sausage nestled inside. The fragrance of warn biscuits wafted up from the box.

"Good, Good," Mr. Dumont beamed. "You there, missy." (He never troubled himself to learn the help's name.) "Take about a dozen of those biscuits and put them away for my breakfast tomorrow. Now do it right now!"

"Hot Damn! That Lela makes the best biscuits in the county! Now missy, you serve the rest as soon as the guests arrive."

He mumbled to himself "Give them bastards a little taste of heaven before they get sloppy drunk."

Helen walked into the dining room. On the table covered with a handmade lace tablecloth sat a huge sheet cake that read "Happy Birthday Darling" in bold letters. It was decorated with mounds of icing, roses, ivy and curly cues. All around the dining room and living room were tiny tables on which crystal dishes were set, filled with mints, pink and green, and various nuts. She continued into the living room. She walked to the French doors that lead to the garden. She mused. This old place was a real mausoleum when I came here. But true to his word, John Lee gave me a free hand to decorate as I please. I got rid of that old-fashioned Duncan Phyfe furniture and got all European furniture. She opened the French doors. The doors opened to an intimate little patio with two white wrought-iron chairs and a table. The banisters and railings on either side of the patio were also white wrought iron. Huge pink and white oleanders stood on each side of the patio. Three steps led down to the garden path which was covered with tiny white rocks. The path lengthened for about thirty feet and then split and curved like an arch. Stone white benches were scattered about the garden, each one shadowed by a crepe myrtle tree displaying its pink blossoms.

The brick wall at the back of the garden was covered with climbing roses. In one comer stood a stately old magnolia tree. In the other corner a fountain bubbled gaily. The statuary was of a young woman with flowing hair with long skirts, pouring water from a jug. The water flowed down three tiers before recycling. The outer garden path was lined with rose bushes of different hues. On opposite sides in the arch were beds of yellow and orange chrysanthemums and calendulas of gold and yellow. Monkey grass covered the area without flowers, with watermelon colored Johnny-jump-ups peeking out.

The side gate which led to the back patio was framed by a trellis covered with red running roses. Tiny white lights were strung through the trees, and fireflies flitting back and forth gave the illusion of an enchanted garden.

Helen never worked in the garden, but often sat in it. She delighted in calling her friends in New York who were bound by snow and ice and telling them about her beautiful Southern garden.

NO HARM DONE - PART 2
Mary Tate

About nine o'clock the guests began to arrive. A few had started the party before leaving home as was easily discernable by the way they greeted the host, with loud guffaws and shrill hellos. The combo had arrived earlier and soon the party was in full swing. They played songs from the Hit Parade and old stuff like Oh, You Beautiful Doll. Moses moved among the guests, serving drinks, taking orders, smiling and speaking politely to those he knew.

"Good evening, Mr. Burt. What can I get for you? Evening Mr. Harry, can I freshen your drink? Evening Mr. Will. Usual drink for you?"

Moses worked fast and furiously, mixing drinks for the guests. As he served the drinks he heard snatches of conversation.

"This integration stuff is a pile of shit! We treat our nigras well, don't we? They satisfied. Ain't that right Moses?" (He did not stop for a reply from Moses.)

"Well I say it's a damn shame to try and mix the races. It ain't healthy," said one of the guests.

Faith, one of the wives, chimed in. "My husband Burt heard our daughter Emmy Lou say that that new negra singer, Johnny Mathis, could put his shoes under her bed any day and he just about had heart failure. Why he wanted to put poor Emmy out of the house. I had to cry and plead and keep my legs open for a week before he calmed down."

"That colored music is disgraceful!" said another guest.

"My maid Matty Mae is a real jewel. We are so close I just Love her to death. But she knows she better not sit her black behind in my living room like company."

The caterers were beginning to set up the portable tables for the sumptuous fare that was to follow. The smell of roast turkey, roast beef and ham began to permeate the area. Potato salad, green salad and broccoli salad appeared, along with several Jello molds in festive colors. There were green beans with almond slivers, English peas served in edible pastry cups, a huge tray of mac and cheese (JL's favorite), several platters of deviled eggs, cracked crab legs on ice in crystal bowls, a shrimp salad mold surrounded by various crackers, cheese, olives, pickles and onions, hot butter rolls, punch and lemon and lime frappe in huge crystal punch bowls with silver ladles. For dessert there would be pound cake and peach ice cream. At the very end of the table was a huge watermelon that had been cut in half and hollowed out. The top half was set up to look like a lid. The bottom half contained various melon balls, strawberries, green and red grapes, pineapple chunks and peach slices. The effect was it looked like a treasure chest with jewels spilling out of it.

By midnight Moses was mixing only highballs. They never knew the difference after midnight anyway.

Helen realized that if she was to have a little fun with the candle blowing ceremony it was now or never. She walked to the middle of the patio, smoothed the white sheath into which she had changed, tossed her auburn hair, called for silence, and invited "all you Southern Gentlemen to help me blow out the candles." Men staggered and stumbled to get a place around the table near Helen.

"Hey Helen, theresh on'ne twenty shisx candlesh on thish cake, Wha' abou' the other four?"

The women giggled, the men guffawed.

"All right, now. Firsh we're all going to shing Happy Birthday Helen, and then we're all going to blow out the candlesh."

Moses, noticing that only legs and posteriors were visible, thought of a football huddle. A shrill voice pierced his thoughts.

"Cut out the dreaming and give me a drink I said. What are you getting paid for anyway?" Moses was shocked back into reality and quickly began mixing a highball.

In the meantime, the circle had broken up and the guests were milling around aimlessly. Helen glanced around, quickly noted that her husband had left the room, rapidly gulped down the last of her martini and announced:

"I'm going to kiss every man in the place."

This brought new spirit to the party as she knew it would. Helen made the rounds smacking at will whoever chanced to be closest, forehead, jaw, cheek, neck, nose. The men laughed and made a big joke of it by ducking or tiptoeing, so that Helen might kiss them where it counted most.

The women were mildly disinterested, disgusted, or envious. They had been through it all before. Moses chuckled to himself.

It ought to be jest about time for Mr. Dumont to make his entrance now, he thought.

When all the male guests had been kissed and a few of the females, (Helen had a sense of humor) she looked around for new worlds to conquer, not willing to let the fleeting sensation of triumph pass so soon. Partly from daring, partly from boredom, perhaps to give them something else to say about the fabulous Helen, "but mostly from the liquor," she announced, "There's one man I haven't kissed yet." She walked with slow fluid movements toward the bartender. There was a stunned silence. Moses, realizing what was about to happen, picked up an ice bucket and quickly walked toward the back porch. Helen stepped between him and the door, hands on hips, head thrown back, a devilish smile on her face. Moses, stupefied, saw two bronze arms extended slowly toward him. Silence. Helen locked her arms around his neck and planted her freshly painted red mouth on Moses' open lips.

The Pain! Terrible! Excrutiating! Then…blackness.

Mr. Dumont had entered and seen his lovely Helen and "him," and something had exploded inside him. He snatched a bottle, a glass, an ashtray, anything to hurt this trespasser with. All of a sudden there he was yelling and screaming and kicking the fallen man.

The rest of the men bolted from their suspension as puppets on strings suddenly jerked into action by a great pair of hands. They rushed to the fallen man, kicked and cursed him without control.

"Dirty dog, kissing Helen like that, who does he think he is. Black bastard!"

"Kill him." "Dirty no good," "Dirty low down…"

The women grouped in corners, afraid, knowing that what the men were doing was wrong but afraid to stop the frenzied actions.

Piercing screams. Helen, her realization now penetrating her liquor, was hysterical. The kicking and swearing stopped almost as abruptly as it had started.

"Help me get her to her room somebody" Mr. Dumont was saying. Stunned silence settled over the group again. All of a sudden the lights looked hideous and the faces distorted from the glow. Everything now seemed stale, used, unreal. Nobody moved. His eyes wandered over the group, and came to rest on the crumbled mass of flesh that still lay on the floor, unmoving. Mr. Dumont looked at it with disgust and hatred. This thing less than a man to him, had received from Helen freely and with pleasure that which she grudgingly allowed to him.

"Call the police and get him out of my sight," Mr. Dumont said through taut lips. He looked at the somber guests, turned quickly on his heels with a finality that set the guests scurrying for the doors, leaving with frantic gestures, the exact opposite of their arrival.

Moses slowly regained consciousness and tried to move but could not. He looked down stupidly at the silver bracelets encircling his wrists. Only then did he realize that he was riding. He raised his eyes slowly from the handcuffs… a screen; on the other side, two silent men in blue uniforms.

Soon Moses was standing in front of the Desk Sergeant and being held up on his feet by his two escorts. Moses caught snatches of what they said, "kissed old man Dumont's wife… ought to be hanged… should have beat him to death… feel like giving him a going over myself." Moses tried to speak. He heard, "shut up you black…" Fury and madness welled up inside him. Almost too weak to stand, he tried to free himself, and was met with a slap across the face.

"Don't get too smart you dirty…

"I have to get free. Got to call Lela. She'll worry. Have to get away from them…

Take him and throw him in a cell" the Sergeant called after them, "and show him how we treat the dogs what don't have no respect for authority, let alone to kiss one of our kind. Ought to be put under the jail."

Moses could feel himself being bodily dragged, then thrown roughly into a cell. "Have to call Lela" he whispered hoarsely. "You ain't calling nobody tonight or ever." Moses made a pleading gesture. "Git your dirty hand off me you…" The large red hand with the signet ring flashed across his mouth. An ivory tooth fell to the floor. Warm, sticky blood from the gaping red hole ran out of his mouth.

My Gawd, hep me. Jesus Lawd hep me. Why Lawd, Why? Why? Why?

Moses struggled to the small hard cot, lowered himself carefully, stretched out and then, mercifully fell into unconsciousness again.

When he finally awoke it was morning. He rose with great difficulty. He ached all over, chest, stomach, head. Moses put his hand to his face, both eyes were swollen almost closed, a tooth was missing and blood was crusted on the temples and forehead from deep gashes there.

My poor Lela, been worried 'bout me all night I know… hate for her to see me like this… don't want to go home like this… Poor Lela, be worried sick… Lawd, I feel so bad…

"Lady to see you and mind you keep your distance. I'll be right here," a voice broke through the haze. Moses looked up and saw beautiful red hair flowing around a face hidden behind dark glasses. She entered his cell wearing a white dress and white four inch pumps.

"Moses, I just came by to tell you I'm sor… I really didn't mean for anything to happen like it did last night. I guess I just didn't realize…" she stopped and looked intently at him.

"God, you look like hell." She paused… a pink tongue darted out and moistened two bright orange lips.

""Well, I'm in a hurry," the voice said uncertainly. "Oh yes, uh, Mr. Dumont says you needn't report for work anymore." Paused again… "I couldn't do anything with him. You can see my position can't you?" the voice continued, "Well, you'll make out. Here, take this." She pressed something into his hand. "You'll make out." She smiled nervously. "I arranged with the officers outside to let you go." She said louder "They're letting you go. Really, there was no harm done." The voice waited, looked, turned and walked quickly away.

---No harm done--- Only when he heard those words did Moses realize she had been talking all this time. Someone came to the cell and turned the key in the lock. Moses walked slowly to the outer door.

"Boy, you mind yourself, you hear? If you ever get in here again, you might not get out so easy," the blue uniform boomed after him.

Moses walked outside. The day was damp and dreary. It started to rain lightly. The words kept ringing in his ears ---no harm done---no harm done---no harm done---

He felt something in his hand. He looked at it; a crisp new twenty-dollar bill... the large hand closed tightly over it and then hung limply at his side. The crumpled green bill fell into the gutter, crushed, misused, getting soggy, no longer what it was meant to be. Then the man, head bent, shoulders stooped, aching, broken, trudged on weary feet into the grayness.

OUT TO THE SYLVESTERS
A Trip to Nostalgia
Mary Tate

It was a warm summer night in Alabama. An old blue Chevy pulled into a gas station and asked for one dollar's "worf a gas." As the two young couples sat laughing while waiting for the gas, a brand-new '54 red Ford drew up. The driver ordered two dollar's "worf a gas." The gas sign read thirty cents a gallon. He glanced over at the Chevy and shouted with glee "Hey, man. Whatsup? Where y'all headed?" "We going out to the Sylvesters' for the annual barn dance." "Is that tonight?" "Sho is. We gon dance the night away." The red Ford passengers talked briefly among themselves. The driver shouted "lead the way. We right behind you." Both cars pulled off down Highway 45 to the Sylvesters' annual barn dance.

The Slylvesters were a prominent family in the area who had once owned a dairy. It was defunct now but the barn was kept in good condition. Once each year Mr. Sylvester opened it up for a dance. It was an annual fund raiser for his church and the social event of the summer. Everybody looked forward to attending.

The couples arrived and drove in between two huge brick pillars with a light on top of each one. Many cars were already there. As there was a lot of land between the big house and the barn they were able to find a parking place without much trouble. They could hear the rock-ola (jukebox) blaring before they got out of their cars. They got out quickly and danced their way to the front entrance to the barn. The entry fee was one dollar per person. The couples entered and began to dance immediately. The huge center aisle of the barn was covered with sweating gyrating dancers. Ladies wore summer dresses with wide swirling skirts. The men wore slacks and short-sleeved shirts. The side stalls were filled with small groups talking, keeping time to the music and eating and drinking. Hot dogs and soda were sold in the tack room, beer and hard liquor in the feed room. Several older church members patrolled the grounds making sure that there was no disturbing the peace, rowdiness or hanky panky going on. The rock-ola was unplugged promptly at two. Everybody left feeling happy and looking forward to next summer when Mr. Sylvester opens the barn for the annual Sylvester Barn Dance.

RHODE ISLAND REDS AND ME
Ardith Thompson

In our large backyard, my mother always kept a flock of chickens. Her favorites were the Rhode Island Reds, a beautiful, reddish-brown breed. I came to love the hens, too, as I listened to their quiet "Cluck, clucks" after they laid their large brown eggs. The rooster wasn't so quiet, though, with his ear-piercing "Cock-a-doodle-doos."

As I scattered seed for the Reds, I noticed one chicken following me, and not just for the grain. I started talking to her and she clucked back. We soon became good friends, and she eventually evolved as my pet. I named her Jill, and we had many happy years talking together, with her being my confidante.

Visitors to our home sometimes were amused to see me carrying around a fowl. But to me she wasn't just a chicken. She was my pet. She finally died of old age one Christmas Day. My mother waited until the next day to tell me so my special day wouldn't be spoiled.

When my father killed a chicken for our Sunday dinner, I was always fearful that Jill would be the next victim. My mother always assured me that my pet would be entirely too tough to eat.

The Rhode Island Reds made up into delicious fricasseed chicken. Since we entertained many guests at dinner, these cut-up pieces of chicken, stewed in stock and served in a white butter sauce, always made a hit. They were served over mashed potatoes, home-grown, of course.

Since Heifers International is a favorite charity of mine, I was happily surprised to see a flock of Rhode Island Reds shown in the catalog. Now, at Christmas time, I donate several flocks of chickens for Third World countries. I tell my grandchildren, to whom I give the gift certificates, that they are in memory of my pet Jill. My recollections of Jill and of all Rhode Island Reds are treasured ones.

TAKING A RISK
Ardith Thompson

I had misgivings when Lucas, my grandson, decided to go to Junipero Serra High School. True, it was in his boundary zone, but it had a reputation for low academic expectations and a lack of school safety control. Lucas could have obtained an inter-district transfer to another school, to one outside our district, or to a private school. I felt it was a big risk to go to Junipero Serra, but Lucas accepted the challenge.

The first thing he did was to enroll in leadership classes. It meant starting school earlier in the mornings than usual, but he never complained. This group did much to promote school spirit. They sponsored contests, parades with floats, homecoming, community service; they were the student government.

Lucas excelled in volleyball and became team captain. He was chosen to be an "athlete of the week." He received awards for academic and athletic excellence. He led his volleyball team to league championship. I would hear him on the phone encouraging his team members to come to practice.

Junipero Serra's constituency is economically distressed. Many of the parents are non-English speaking. For most of Lucas' games, he would be the only one having parents in attendance. Although there is a dedicated staff and the school has a well-controlled environment, nearly half of the senior class did not qualify for graduation.

Now it was graduation night. I'm sure Lucas did not think back at all to his first few months at Junipero Serra, when he was robbed twice. We had excellent seats and noticed him marching in and sitting in one of the reserved seats on the stage. He was wearing an honor medal, as had his four cousins who had previously graduated from El Cerrito High.

I remember when my firstborn grandchild marched in sixteen years ago. A lady next to me had said, "Are you going to cry?" I said, "Probably." Now I had the same emotions. I hadn't known Lucas was to be one of the speakers. At six feet, two inches, he towered above the other participants. The sea of red and gold gowns on the floor and stage was impressive.

Lucas' speech was based on the quote: "If you have faith as small as a mustard seed, you can say to this mountain, 'Move from here to there and it will move.' Nothing will be impossible for you." There was much applause after the talk. A woman behind me said, loudly, "Amen!"

As president of the student association, Lucas helped to call out names of those receiving diplomas. My own "cup" was full and overflowing. I'm so glad my fifth grandchild, Lucas Edward Lipscomb, took the risk and attended Junipero Serra.

LOVE
Bola Thompson

True love, discovered
Next to me at the banquet
Then I met his wife.

LEGACY OF A WANDERER: THE GUITAR PLAYING MAN
Terrance Touchett

In a Western town called "No Name," which was in a deserted grassland of Texas, a dilapidated saloon stood among deserted buildings along a dusty road which passed through "No Name."

Inside the saloon an aged cattleman named Jaw Bones Jack Borna sat on a wooden stool with his guitar set on his lap. His slender body was slumped over the guitar. He was in the senior years of his life of long drives of cattle to grazing lands far from his "No Name" hometown, now deserted in the over-grazed cattle ranges.

While sitting on his stool in the saloon, stooped over his guitar, Jack Borna closed his eyes. In his dream he wondered if anyone remembered cattle moving along the range, and the joys of the cowboys sitting around night fires while playing their guitars and singing about their freely roaming life.

As he dreamed he further wondered if he'd pass on the memories of the free open air life, as his heritage to some wrangler who would sing to guitar songs about the free wandering days, or would everything be lost and buried in his grave.

In Jack's dream he spured his quarter horse, galloping it into the herd pasturing in the grazing lands. As he galloped his horse he screamed, "Trail herd ho! Round 'em up! Move 'em out! Cowboys ride!"

Cowboys sang out along with Jack:

Chip, pa, de clap! Clip, pa, de clap!
We'll ride through this dusty drive.
Clip, pa, de, clap!

Jack sang back:

For cowboy you gotta fight to survive or you'll die. Drive 'em out! Push 'em out! For there's a long way to water.

Cowboys sang out along with Jack:

Ride, ride, ride, ride, ride, ride!
Ride cowboys ride! We'll fight to survive.
We'll fight the demon rustlers thundering along the fuming sky.
So spur our horses and ride to survive.

Jack sang out while spuring his horse:

> *Drive 'em hard! Rope in those mavericks!*
> *Search for water. We aim to survive.*

Cowboys galloped alongside of the herd while shouting:

> *Somewhere there's water. But today there's not a cloud in sight.*

Jack answered their shouting:

> *A cowboy's only relief is when she sings, "Get along cattle we've got a long ways to water! Round 'em up! Keep 'em going. Beware cowboys, stampedes are the demon rustler's deed."*

Out of the daze of his dream, Jack shook his head when he heard the saloon's swing doors open from gusts of wind that twirled along the saloon floor. Dust and tumbleweeds flew around the stool which Jack was slouched over. As the wind died down, he fell asleep dreaming about the excitement while he drove the herd nearer to other pasture lands.

A bush of tumbleweed slapped against his legs, resting on the saloon floor, creeping from the wind, twirling the dried bush out the saloon's swinging doors. All this commotion awoke Jack from out of his sleep. He stood up to kick the tumbleweed out of his legs. As he swung around, his body shook energetically with them. He grabbed his guitar and strummed an arousing tune to awaken the drovers and barmaids, now drunk and slumped over the saloon floor.

> *Drink the cold brew,*
> *Before the devil burns up your belly.*
> *Drink it up my friends,*
> *And let the demons have the tomorrows.*
> *Drink! Drink to forget your sorrows.*
> *Drink!*
>
> *For it's beer, whisky, and stink'n cigars.*
> *So bring on the petty-coated women.*
> *For there's plenty of life in this old carcass*
> *Howl, dee old lady hee,*
> *Howl dee old lady oh,*
> *Oldee, oldee, oldee lady oh.*

*I'll howl for my lady oh,
Lady, lady, lady, oh!*

*Prairie dust covers my boots.
Calluses stiffen my hands.
The bank's calling my notes,
And my herds drop'n dead on my mortgaged land.
Now my kids are feel'n the pain.
Oh, when are we gonna get some rain?
Till then:*

*What do I have to fear?
I've been down this road before.
As long as there's my horse under me,
And as long as there's beer at the bar,
I'll be doggone if I'm going anywhere.*

Jack stepped to the middle of the saloon floor, stamped down his foot and sang out:

*Clasp your partner for the Round House Reel.
Shuffle along two by two, circling about to the left.
Forward one and down the center. Now it's back home again.*

*Men step forward to lead. Ladies from the caboose.
Sound the alarm, Toot! Toot! Toot!
Stop at the village station. Passengers come aboard.
All aboard for the Round House Reel.*

*Chug, chug along again my friends.
Up the mountain, and down again, picking up speed.
Around the slopes we go.
Winding round and round.
Slow her down. Stop at the watering tank.
Drink up and that's the Round House Reel. Reel. Reel.*

The rumpus of the swinging beat of the guitar playing man's music, dancing, romping, and the bar room commotion blasted its sound out the swinging saloon's doors. It swung out onto the town's street once in dead silence of the deserted "No Name" town.

The clouds in the night sky fogged away the sight of the saloon and the music of the guitar playing man.

Outside the saloon a young boy stepped along the creaking wood sidewalk along the street leading toward the saloon. The boy looked up as he was attacked by the sound of the guitar playing man's music inside the saloon. He stepped toward the saloon. He leaned under the door.

As the boy peeked from under the saloon door into the saloon, he saw Jack slumped back on his stool after finishing his song. Asleep, Jack again dreamed back to his youth.

Jack dreamed about a long time ago. He envisioned back in the saloon. He was seated on his stool with his guitar in his hand.

> *He created the commotion, singing in motion,*
> *Pick'n and strumm'n the music of the guitar playin man.*
> *Creating the music for his one-man band.*
> *Hope'n and praying to play*
> *In the big city band one mile down the road.*
> *Creating the commotion, singing in motion,*
> *Pick'n, strumm'n the music of the guitar playing man.*

> *He played the music fast and then he played it slow.*
> *Swung it to a do si do.*
> *One tune sung into the next.*
> *His fingers knew all the strumm'n tricks.*
> *It was all that anyone could do*
> *To keep track of his strumm'n fingers.*
> *Dancing along that silvery string guitar*
> *As the people danced in front of him.*

As Jack dreamed on, the boy stepped back onto the sidewalk and whispered "I'd like to be someday a guitar playing man!"

> *Each night the lad returned to hear*
> *The music of the guitar play'n man.*
> *Then one day the boy approached the saloon.*
> *Setting there on a stool was the guitar.*
> *On it a note was hung,*

"Closed and gone to rest one mile down the road.
See that my guitar makes it, as I couldn't
To that singing and swinging city down the road."
This lad picked up the guitar the way down the road
To that stoneless grave of the guitar playing man.
Then he fulfilled the guitar playing man's wish

When he stopped at the mound, where the guitar playing man was laid to rest in his grave, the boy stood before the grave. He strummed the guitar, and whispered "Now I'm the guitar playing man."

From the echoes out of the canyon below the grey wolves howled. Crying away the passing of Jaw Bones Jack Borna. Still playing his guitar, he headed back to the saloon. Upon arriving back in "No Name," he swung the saloon doors open. As he stepped inside the patrons raised their mugs. Their voices shouted out a toast to the lad, now the new guitar playing man.

The lad strummed his guitar and...
Created the motion,
Singing in motion
Pick'n and strumming
The music of the guitar playing man.

The clouds in the sky darkened. Rain poured down, and a mist shadowed away "No Name" town to the big city in the sky.

THE SOUND OF HUMANITY
Terrance Touchett

The cracking of breaking glass pierced the darkness along the alley of this rundown section of Harper's Ferry. No one in the sleeping town ventured out to check on the source of the intrusion on their silence. Not a light turned on from any of the shanty back porches. Not an eye peeked through the rag-curtained windows.

The rattling of a garbage can, followed by a thud, broke the silence. Growling sounds came from the side of the house. If anyone had been watching, they would have seen a person wiggle into a window. As he fell into the house he landed with another thud.

"Damn," he cursed as he rose off the floor. He was in the bedroom of the house. Rubbing his head, which had smacked onto the hardwood floor, he switched on his flashlight to regain his bearing.

As he hastily advanced toward the dresser, he slipped on something that sent him falling on his backside. For a moment he lay stunned and groaning. As he pushed himself up from the floor by grabbing the side of the bed, the railing collapsed. His head hit the bedpost. Stumbling sideways, he bounced off the wall and clutched the dresser. His groans grew louder.

The man and the dresser began to slide across the floor right into the open closet. The door slammed shut with the dresser and the wretched soul inside. As he turned to review the situation, he bumped an overhead shelf. The contents of the shelf dumped onto him. Now he was covered with open-toed shoes. A brassiere and a black slip lay draped on his head.

Finally, his anger erupted. The dresser burst out of the door shattering the hinges. He bolted after it and let forth a resounding "Grr." Now he lay atop the dresser which was parked on the bed.

He jerked up, whirled in all directions as if to challenge the dresser, closet and all else that would cause him any more trouble. Then he jumped off the bed and bellowed another turbulent "Grr."

As he strutted through the bedroom door, a gust of wind came through and slammed the door shut right in his face. He spun around cockeyed. His body swayed. Then he tensed up straight as a rocket. He drew back and flung himself through the door, shattering it. Like a rocket he flashed across the hallway, straight through a screen door, off the back porch and into a garbage can.

Sounds of "Grr" echoed from inside this steel coffin while he pounded and kicked in a frenzy causing the contents of the can to decorate his body.

Just then a car turned into the yard. Its lights spotted the disarrayed scene. By this time he was engulfed in the garbage can bombarding it against a helpless maple tree in a desperate effort to be released from the shackles of this tormentor.

A woman parked her car, and she and several children dashed over to him. The woman screamed, "Oscar! What happened?" Rotating his turret toward the voice, he calmed to a mild tremor.

His wife surveyed the scene and asked innocently, "Didn't you see my note? I left the back door open for you."

Silence loomed ominously around this knight in tarnished armor. Then the tremor rose. He stamped his feet. The muscles in his arms twitched against the garbage can like gongs in a bell. Through the dust rising about him, his angry growling grew in intensity, and finally exploded into a full-scale scream. He went rushing down the street, now full of neighbors who had been awakened by the clamor. This was war!

The woman stood motionless and sighed, "I don't think he found my note."

HAVE A GREAT DAY
Terrance Touchett

HAVE A GREAT DAY!
There are many more days to come.
The sun is shining on your smiling face.
Why cry when there can be so much fun?
There's neighborliness where you are.
Families are cheering greetings to everyone.

HAVE A GREAT DAY!
Let nothing worry you, everything's fine.
Beauty can be seen near and far.
Flowers in bloom with colors blazing in the sun.
Sweetheart couples gaze at each other.
See and live each day proudly.

HAVE A GREAT DAY!
Everything's fine between you and me.
You'll always have friends encouraging feelings.
Together days are full of happiness.
You will know many more happy days.

HAVE A GREAT DAY!
There are loving people hugging everywhere.
Moms and dads caress their kids.
Puppies and cats lick each other.
Birds chirp to their chicks in their nest.
Skies are blue, clouds puff along leisurely.

HAVE A GREAT DAY!
Live each day proudly and lightly.
Days flow by in full greatness.
More days for sharing our love.
Everything's fine between you and me.
Sing! Shout! Live it up!

A SHOPPING I'LL GO
Terrance Touchett

Oh, deploring housework
With duties to wash and dry.
Floors to scrub, wax and shine,
Windows to clean until sparking.
And dishes to fill this darn machine.
And not to forget to microwave my frozen dinner.

Home and school meetings are tomorrow.
But maybe I can think of something else to do.

Oh boring wife work
My tasks are never done.
Such is it my responsibility to do ____ or ____
Or nosey neighbors will whisper gossip.
There's got to be more to life than these daily tasks.
Who needs a budget?
Everything is chargeable!
The national economy depends on spending.
The American dollar needs to be spent!
Sales ____ cents off ____ deals ____ coupons!

CIRCUS
Terrance Touchett

Sticky candy, sweet ice cream,
Sausages in a bun for everyone.
Hey, one and all, hear my call,
It's circus time.

Pony rides for the kids,
Flowers and pretty aprons for Mom,
And contests with prizes for Dad.
Come on! It's circus time.

Don't miss the exhibits of wonder,
A lady fatter than a hog,
A fire-eating man,
And a two-headed calf, gads!
It could only happen at circus time.

You'll be amazed and surprised,
Here at the greatest circus of all.
It's a once in a lifetime adventure.
So get your tickets for all the shows.

Circus time! Circus time!
Step right up to circus time!

SLEEPLESS NIGHTS
Anke Van Aardenne

Sleepless nights
thoughts spin
around in my mind
too active to sleep
endless streams
pleasant memories
scary memories
unsettling memories
try to relax
counting is of no help
disturbing thoughts appear
sudden bursts of energy
like a cat
running to escape a dog
a flash of inspiration
a warm bed to share
soon two bodies sleep
intertwined and innocent

RURAL HOLLAND
Anke Van Aardenne

Grazing cows in lush meadows
carpeted with abundant grasses
rain occurs
reflecting like diamond drops

Farms with straw thatched roofs
sheltering animals during winter
cows bellow–milking time
farmers busy with preparations

Cows stand in neat rows
milking machines are hooked up
milk streaming into buckets
transferred to the dairy factory

Smell of freshly cut grass
scenting the air
tracks from machines
leaving marks in the meadows
huge zigzag labyrinths

Harvesting corn
row after row
drying in the shed
winter food
until spring arrives
and they graze outside

ROOM WITH A SKELETON
Anke Van Aardenne

I went to primary and high school in Dordrecht, the Netherlands. My primary school was located in the center of town. The school, called the "Hof School," was and still is an old red brick building with square windows and with a lion-gated portal to enter the double doors leading into the hallways. Once inside you encounter a stairway going to the second floor. The classrooms are located on both sides of the hallways. The fenced yard is on the other side of the school. I lived about a twenty- minute walk away from the school and I, like almost all of the other children, walked to school.

I'd like to tell you about an incident I have never forgotten which occurred when I was in fifth grade.

My schoolmates and I played hop-scotch during lunchtime outside on the playground. It was almost time to get back to our classrooms when I heard the headmaster's whistle. It meant it was time to line up two by two in a neat procession. Every class had to line up in similar fashion. The schoolyard looked as if an army drill sergeant had given orders. Each class stood in separate lines. Small first graders followed their teacher across the barren, brick-paved playground as obedient as chicks following their mother to the hen house. In order of grade level each class walked inside the school. I became impatient from the wait and talked to my friend. With the exuberance of a fifth grader I could not stand perfectly still while waiting endlessly, so it seemed to me, for all the lower grade classes to march inside. I became impatient and talked to a friend next to me. Finally, our teacher, Mr. Hoekstra, blew his whistle as a sign for our class to march inside. We ascended, still neatly two by two, the seven gray marble steps to enter the old school building while we marched along the long marble hallway and turned right. We came to a stone staircase, twisting and curving while it went upwards. Mr. Hoekstra saw me step out of line at a certain moment (I had not followed the identical path as the person ahead of me) and immediately called out my name, "Anna, come here. You are not following the school rules. I will send you to the storage room so you can reflect on the necessity of obeying the rules."

He told the class to take their seats and turned to me. I had to follow him to a dimly lit storage room. He got out his black metal key chain and after a few tries he found the key to open the door. We both entered the poorly lit, dusty room that would become my prison.

"You'll have to stay here to reflect on your behavior till it is time to go home. I will come to unlock the door after all the children have left the school grounds. I hope you will learn from this experience!" With those words he locked me in the stuffy dimly lit room and left to teach my classmates.

I felt furious because in my opinion I was innocent. I was a lively ten-year-old girl who had danced a bit out of line. Was that such a crime? I could see no justice in this severe punishment.

I sat on the only wooden chair and after a while climbed up on it to observe through the high window the schoolyard. I saw the square of the playground. A huge brick wall encircled the whole yard. We tossed our balls against this wall. On top of the wall was iron netting, undoubtedly to prevent our balls from flying into neighboring yards. Dark green ivy had slowly invaded the iron netting, giving it the only life that existed in the yard when it was not populated by the students. I often wondered why there were no trees planted on our playground. It was such a barren environment.

Small yards lined the fence. I was amazed at the difference in appearance of those yards. There were yards with a big apple tree, yards with only grass, yards with carefully manicured vegetable gardens, yards with a rose garden and an old white wooden bench and a bird bath, one yard was completely overgrown with weeds, as tall as I was, where I saw birds landing. It would be nice to play hide-and-seek in this one, I thought.

After a while I became bored looking outside. Now I focused on the room I was in. It was used as a storage room. The walls were covered with dusty files in metal racks. I could not remember seeing one person enter or exit this room as long as I had attended school. It seemed to me a place of death.

In one corner was a sheet-covered object. My curiosity won and as I approached I lifted gently and slowly the dust-covered white sheet. With a cry of terror I stood face to face with a human skeleton. A huge black spider had made the ribcage its home. The interior cavity had a shiny, silvery glow of the web; it was still softly moving by the air movement of the discarded sheet. I trembled with fear as I listened for footsteps of my teacher approaching down the hallway. He might have heard my cry. I kept very quiet but heard no footsteps. All I saw was this huge black spider climbing up in the cavity. For the first time ever I stood face to face with a skeleton. I felt very uneasy and a bit scared.

Once this used to be a person, a real live person like me, I thought. This thought kept racing through my mind. I am not alone in this room but with the skeleton remains of a dead person and a live spider. I was frightened but at the same time reassured. I started to look at my own body and find the comparable bones in the skeleton. The pelvic area was a mystery to me. Those white blades sticking out were the pelvic bones I thought. They circled around and I fantasized that this would be a female skeleton and the white blades used to hold and protect her babies.

Suddenly I heard the four o'clock bell ringing. I covered the skeleton as fast as I could and sat down on the only wooden chair in the room. I soon heard many echoing footsteps passing and a lot of talking and laughing as my schoolmates were leaving to go home.

Finally, there were no more sounds in the school or yard, so now Mr. Hoekstra will come soon to unlock me, I happily thought. I possessed no watch so all I could do was to wait; maybe he is doing some paperwork before he comes to unlock me, I thought as I waited and waited. It was starting to get dark. He must have forgotten all about locking me up in this room and I will be here forever and ever. I know my parents will get worried that I'm not home yet. Surely they will go to my friend to ask her if she knows where I am. Then they will come and rescue me. With courage in my heart after this thought my endless wait continued.

Suddenly I could hear someone whistling. I heard sounds of running water and splashing sounds. This must be the janitor cleaning up and washing down the floors, I thought. With all my might I bounced on the door and yelled: "Get me out, please let me out of here."

"I am coming, I am coming," I heard the janitor reply.

It was followed by the familiar sound of a key turning in the lock and the door flew open.

"Why are you in here?" the janitor asked, perplexed. "I have been locked up since the afternoon classes started," I sobbed to the janitor. "I want to go home; my parents will be very worried."

A bewildered janitor saw me run past him down the hallway and the stairs towards my freedom of the darkening street.

I have no recollection of how my parents handled this situation.

In later years I wondered if my parents ever talked to the school principal and if Mr. Hoekstra had been reprimanded. I have no recollection of that, only a very bad memory of that day.

MUST SAY GOOD-BYE
Barbara Akosua Williams

Time to say good-bye
certainly was not prepared
how do I prepare to say good-bye to youth
no grandchildren as a reminder
no prom to celebrate menopause
no gray hair
the hormones know and they stop
the body responds naturally
my mind struggles
not prepared for this half way point
no one values these wrinkles that are creeping in
i can stick to the *you are as young as you feel* line
but this body knows
the hormones know

i don't want to know
but i know

so i take these pills replacing nature
i know
so i trick my body
cannot trick my mind
life begins at forty
what happens at fifty
the hormones know
so once again i am at a Y in the road of life
which path to take
a new life …a new me…
or just bury my dreams
too late

so i grieve the passage of the girl,
the young woman,
the middle-aged woman
i hug her

i kiss her
i miss all of the hers
i release her as slowly as a mother releases a child
i look in the mirror at the woman staring back

i reach to the source that has guided and protected
the girl
the young woman,
the middle-aged woman

VISITS
Barbara Akosua Williams

some called him crazy
I called him Dad
visiting him in sad places
seeing through the madness
sitting with the proud warrior
bearing witness to love
now I visit his spirit
basting in our love
some called him crazy
I called him Dad

SOMETIMES
Barbara Akosua Williams

Sometimes
it just plain hurts
never stopped wanting that family love thing
always the same results
just cannot give them enough
never enough of whatever they want
whenever I say no more
all that was given is forgotten
I am scorned again.
Sometimes
it just plain hurts

Therapy, twelve-step program, prayers
nothing could stop
the giving and hurting

I just keep on giving
it seems
expectations is the problem
just don't expect much
not even a thank you
Sometimes
it just plain hurts

I retreat to my cave
surrounded by walls of activity
safety in the illusion of separation
pretend I do not need them
find peace in the aloneness
Sometimes
it just plain hurts

EXPLORATIONS IN EQUITY
Barbara J. Williams

On a balmy day in San Francisco, USA
All the automated people are not aware.
They wish life was not so hectic, in a way,
But to really hope for change they do not dare.

I wish that they could all know what I know
And see a simple way of life could be,
where the " rat race" as a way of life would go,
and we would know what is "society."

Society is what we do together
And not an alien force or upper class.
Society should be pleasant like good weather,
And let us have time to sit upon the grass.

Each of us could trust our natural feelings
If the powers that control us would allow.
Instead we are molded to be like others,
So we lose the very sense of who we are.

It is a vicious circle and we are kind of driven

The momentum doesn't leave us time to think.
We need to stop and feel how we are driven,
Before we die of ulcers or pollution's stink.

The symptoms seem to strike a kind of terror
We know that our society is sick,
But no one seems to see the basic error
Which makes things tick the way they tick.

It is a system which promotes confusion,
By controlling minds and confiscating wealth.
There is one big and grand delusion
With which we all deceive ourselves.

The earth is priceless and needed by us all,
And yet we buy and sell and hope to profit
From a thing we cannot claim except by law.
How is it that the value keeps increasing
Each time a place on this earth changes hands?

Could it be that what is done on land has value?
And that the value of the land remains the same.
The roads and schools are not provided by the landlord.
There seems to be a great deal of confusion.
Rent and taxation need examination rather than blame.

We might separate the public from the private
And keep them both intact with equity.
Some thinking has been done already
In a book by Henry George called Progress and Poverty.

We are all victims of the same delusion.
There is no class of people we can blame.
Each one of us contributes to the misery.
The blight upon us all is just the same.

The system pits us one against the other
And creates the means to build monopoly.
MONOPOLY--Why that is a game we are playing.
When will we wake up and see?

It's fear that keeps us grasping for and grabbing what we can.
Opportunities grow less and less for every man.
A government should serve the public interest,
And not meddle in private lives.

Taxation is the "rack" on which we are stretched until we hurt.
Could it be the evil we need to look at first??
The government which allows this rip-off is ours to keep or change.
The energy crisis I see is mostly in our brains.

When taxes are abolished and rent goes where it's earned,
Monopoly of unused land surely will be spurned
When fair we are required to be we'll know congenial life.
The time is soon a'coming when we will see an end to strife.

JOY
Barbara J. Williams

Joy I have discovered is a quality within.
It's a matter of perceiving as we go through thick and thin.

It is what we ought to feel as we find out who we are,
And learn to share the me in us with others near and far.

It is a dynamic process of fully living life,
Of accepting our ambivalence as a constructive kind of strife.

It is knowing that we are endowed with a Creative Power
To function as a person every day and every hour.

It is awareness to appreciate and freedom to make a choice.
It is giving right to everyone the Thou in them to voice.

Joy is not a destination but a feeling that we know.
It is a state of Being and a way in which we go.

NEW YEAR'S EVE AT THE SENIOR CARE UNIT
Barbara J. Williams

Tonight is New Year's Eve: 1999. Just another night at the skilled nursing facility where I earn my bread-and-butter. "The natives are restless," as the saying goes. Mrs. G is yelling "Hee-eelp!" over and over again. I sang her a lullaby, gave her Thorazine and Benadryl, hugged her and kissed her good-night and still she yells… "Hee-eelp!" I silently count to ten. "Mrs. G, why are you yelling?"

"Because I want to yell." She's been changed, dried, turned and talked to and—wait a minute… she's quiet now. It's 1:30 a.m, I've been here since 11:00.

Meanwhile, on the Alzheimers Unit:

All this time, Bill H., all dressed and ready to go, has been pacing… determined to go "home," to unhitch his horses from the wagon and put them in the barn. He won't open the door because he dislikes the piercing shriek of the alarm. He says nobody has a right to keep him here. He didn't sign himself in, and he's not a crook. He dislikes his roommate because Mr. C. sometimes pees and defecates on the floor by mistake, and talks nonsense and frequently gets in the wrong bed. The fact that Bill is still pacing indicates that the medication I gave him two hours ago has had no effect. Trying not to "get hostile," with me, he wants to "make a deal" with me.

But first: Mae is awake. Doris is awake. Mae will settle down with a hug and milk and a graham cracker. Doris will stay awake no matter what. Betty Jo just wheeled her lopsided hemiparetic self out for her nightly milk and crackers. Keeping an eye on Bill, I become aware that as custodian of demented minds in functional bodies, my heart frequently aches. And my patience wears. But I welcome the opportunity to bring my creative ingenuity into play. Right now, my ingenuity manages to convince him that the horses that he "left outside this afternoon" are sleeping peacefully. At least he's quieter now, though he may be up all night.

Last time I worked here, things were more calm. Everyone slept, or mostly everyone. When I passed medicines that morning I had some good chuckles. Mrs. W and Mrs. H. filled their beds with excrement and after they were cleaned up I gave them their pills and a big hug for good measure. Mrs. W said, "Wait a minute. Let me get my arms out of these covers." I said, "Everybody needs a hug," and she said, "That isn't all they need. There's a guy out in the hall I'd sure like to get in my bed."

When I got to Mrs. P. (she's 97) after I took her pulse and gave her a heart pill and a glass of juice, she said what she says every morning: "You're going to get me drunk." She has an attention-getting habit. So, if you ever go to her room, look carefully where you intend to walk. Because you might step in some little round balls of what looks like chocolate. She produces it and then throws it out of her bed. Sometimes it's neat, and sometimes she needs a bath and complete bed change.

I must remind myself, again and again, to look beyond Mrs. P's persistent tests of my own sanity and patience. I must be mindful that, beyond her frustrating parts, she is still a whole person. In fact…now that I think of it… just last night, somewhere between "get-me-drunk" and "little-round-balls," she gave me a deeper, and most rational, perspective on the unfolding psycho-drama. She reminded me. "We all come here for just one thing, you know that as well as I."

Now it's 3:00 a.m. Back in Room 8, everyone is awake. Bill is still insisting he just arrived here this afternoon. I even took him out for a walk to show him there weren't any horses. It was so chilled and windy that we only walked a half block and back. Now he's saying, "I guess it's too late for the horses. I should never have left them, but I thought I'd only be here 15 minutes."

Endnote: As I drove from the parking lot, I reminded myself to drive carefully. After all, the roads were full of revelers weaving their way home after that party-of-all-parties: the one that began in one century and ended in the next.

MOTHER'S LAMBS
Barbara J. Williams

It was Monday, February 19, 2001, a day of intermittent rain and dramatic skies, filled with all shades of cumulus clouds and reluctant sunshine. I had just worked 3 graveyard shifts at Marin County Psych Emergency. I had even commuted on Sunday so I could attend a memorial tribute for my mother at our church in Grass Valley. It had been wonderful and worth the effort.

Heading home to Grass Valley on Route 37 I ran into a roadblock. Oh well, I will get to go through Napa and Sonoma to reach I 80. As tired as I was, it would still be invigorating to go a different way. First I saw a rainbow, a lovely omen for spiritual wonder. As I drove on, the brilliant green of the vineyards and the startling yellow of mustard flowers thrilled me and the weather continued to give more sunshine and gradually clearing blue sky.

My eyes were roving all over the place and on the right side I saw a large field with sheep. A large black-faced ewe stood over a small black figure. A baby lamb! How precious! I kept going but was drawn back. Turning around, I drove to the spot and parked, to see if I could get a picture. Getting out of my car, I walked across the busy highway to stand by the drainage ditch and study this scene. Mama Ewe was watching me like a hawk. A farmer came out to see what I was looking at and waved, then went to get some feed for this bringer of new life. It became apparent there were two babies and when she turned to eat the food they raised their heads and I got the picture. It was a fertile moment, a haiku moment. As I pulled away I began to cry. For a few minutes I let the healing waters flow over me as I felt the joy and pain of life and how birth and death are all part of it. Soon I began to compose some words for this serendipitous gift of a mystical healing moment.

A week ago my mother died

Today I saw two newborn lambs

And cried.

AUGUST IN PARIS
Valena M. Williams (Sr.)

The newspaper slid to the floor as I grabbed the telephone that morning. Within moments I was talking with a travel agent, nodding excitedly and repeating my credit card number. I was responding to a tiny ad in the Travel Section of the morning paper: two inches, small type, all-black type. "Five days in Paris this week .... on your own... direct roundtrip air fare ... private apartment accommodations in the 1st Arondissment... Metro pass......all for $350."

Before retirement I had taken half a dozen business trips to Paris and felt familiar with the city. Although I hadn't used it I had always admired the pubic transportation. The designated apartment was close to the center of things, a safe and easy location to get around from. This was a steal, so cheap because most Parisians take their six-week holiday to the south of France during July and August. I imagined long leisurely hours for me in less crowded museums. I tried to interest someone else in going but no one could be free on such short notice. I was going by myself to Paris day after tomorrow!

What to wear? Weather in Paris is like San Francisco's. Summer nights last forever, never getting black-dark. I would travel in a simple silk suit and sensible heels. I fit everything I needed into a carry-on, carefully re-checking it. I would be alone but I could be chic. I could wear something other than basics. I tossed the loafers aside, replacing them with a second pair of heels and added a smashing silk dress I had never worn. Everything fit into my carry-on. I was ready.

My family wasn't surprised at my hasty decision because I traveled a lot since retiring. In April I celebrated my eightieth birthday on a cruise to Brazil and was already ticketed for an off-season trip to Crete in the fall. At the airport my daughter teased me: "Shall we just park here and wait?....it's such a short trip."

SFO to JFK to CDG on Air France – the flight went smoothly. The five-course haute cuisine dinner with a second pour of cabernet was served on china with cloth napkins. Sipping brandy I watched the movie The Dancer Upstairs and fell asleep wondering if I would be staying in a studio as sparse as the one in the film.

Six hours later the morning wake-up was followed by a croissant and coffee. It prepared me for the flight attendant's announcement, first in French and then in careful English:

"It is August, 3, 2003. The time is 8:30 am, Central European Time. We will be landing shortly in Paris at Charles de Gaulle Airport where the temperature is an unusual 36°....."

I stopped listening. Thirty-six degrees! That sounded downright cold. I reached for the cardigan in my carry-on. The terminal didn't seem chilly. Then a sign at the bottom of the escalator translated the temperature from the local Celsius into my familiar Fahrenheit. Already it was above 90° outside! I stuffed the sweater back into my suitcase and headed for the nearby Metro. The new euro notes didn't feel French. I missed the francs.

I fumbled for my Metro pass and moved quickly to wait in line. Someone behind me muttered an unfriendly "Une Americaine, bien sur."* Suddenly I felt very alone, almost apprehensive. I knew the war in Iraq was stirring up strong anti-American feelings. Should I even be here?

The easy-to-follow map in the Metro restored my confidence. The Louvre, the Rodin Musée, the Pompidou were very accessible and surely wouldn't be crowded. Empty seats on the Metro were a further good sign. When I got off and started walking, I wished immediately for the loafers I hadn't packed. The search for my address on Rue Ste Martin stretched to several long blacks. My so-called sensible pumps were killing me.

Stumbling at last into a stuffy ground floor office, I was handed a key by a lone desk clerk who checked my reservation and pointed me to the stairs. He shook his head when I asked about an elevator and didn't offer to carry my luggage. I trudged up three steep dark wood-paneled flights, each narrow landing hotter than the last. At the top I unlocked the door and heat rushed out like an oven.

Sweat dripped from me as I kicked off my shoes and opened windows. No air-conditioning. Parisians, like San Franciscans, have a summer grin-and-bear-it attitude about occasional hot weather but to me this lack of air-conditioning seemed just another rejection of American know-how.

I knew I would probably like the woman who lived here. I admired her taste in art, her books, the rugs, the arrangement of simple modern furniture. There was no TV. No computer. She probably took her laptop with her. Small copper pots gleamed in the tiny kitchen but the refrigerator wasn't working. She must use only a mobile*. There was no phone. A fan in the corner promised relief until I realized there was no power. No ice cubes, no air? Perhaps she economized by shutting off the electricity while she was on vacation. Was the small flashlight on the table meant to be a nightlight? Too hot to go downstairs to ask the clerk, I peeled off the damp clothes I had traveled in.

My heart sank as I unpacked. The only cottons in my suitcase were my pajamas.

After a long, cooling shower I spread a quilt on the floor and lay down to wonder what I had gotten myself into. Should I just turn around and go home, no matter what it cost? Or was this worth a try? After all, it was only for five days. I fell asleep waiting for evening when it might be cool enough to get something to eat and something better to wear.

At twilight I dressed to go out. The suit I traveled in was no longer damp. I slid into the pair of Crocs* I had brought along to wear as slippers, just as I wore them at home. They were magic! The holes let my feet breathe and I could walk easily in the cushioning soles. I clunked down the stairs, self-consciously wearing bright pink plastic clogs.

Dark windows held *EN VACANCE** signs but two shops remained open – a little sidewalk café and a neighborhood boulangérie* An espresso and a crunchy baguette prepared me to go looking for hot-weather clothes and loafers.

I took the Metro to a Le Printemps, pleased to find the department store murkily air-conditioned. The shoe clerk noticed my Crocs. She had read about them but they had not yet arrived at European stores. I let her try mine on. When she offered to buy them, even to exchange them for a pair of loafers, I decided I would keep wearing them. They were a novelty, a different sort of fashion statement. I bought and put on a jeans skirt and a washable pink shirt — to match the Crocs.

Outside again, my spirits continued to rise when I saw McDonald's familiar golden arches. *The Croque McDo** with wine was nothing like home. This was a whole new Paris for me. Other times here I had whisked from offices to hotels and had eaten in fine restaurants. Now I wandered through the neighborhoods, sat in sidewalk cafes, prowled through tiny little stores. In the dusk the temperature eased to a tolerable 80° or so. As in New York, people were always on the street. I stayed with them, reluctant to climb up to my stuffy apartment at the end of the day.

Thursday, Friday, and Saturday were a torrid blur with mid-day temperatures soaring to 104°. Each morning the aroma of baking bread tempted me downstairs to sit at the café with a croissant or beignet and café au lait before starting that day's Metro jaunt. On the boulevards I watched chic patrons dash from air-conditioned hotel foyers to air-conditioned cars, just as I had at other times. Sometimes I joined other adults who splashed in the fountains with children. I practiced my French and they laughed when I sang a silly parody I made to the tune of April in Paris: *"Aout in Paris, baked like a baguette, je suis une pomme frite, un grillons ris de veau...."**

Keeping an eye out for nearby pissoirs* I drank bottle after bottle of Evian. Heat radiated from the powerful bronze statues at Le Musee Rodin   The Louvre was air-conditioned but the temperature rose in the humid galleries. But no one jostled or hurried me. This trip lived up to its promise. Everywhere my Crocs caused comment.

On the Left Bank I played chess with a man who spoke no English and smiled as he called me *"une jolie Americane."** When I finally signalled "checkmate" he bought me a sticky *bête du Papa** to match my shoes.

My Walkman was filled with BBC reports of a widespread European heat wave. Some elderly people, left behind by vacationing families, had died right here in Paris. I hoped my family wouldn't be aware of what was happening. They would worry about me. I was worried about myself. Whom would I reach for if I needed help?

I lingered under majestic old trees in the parks and envied naked statues in the Tuilleries. In early evening I sought the cooling marble benches below *Les Invalides*, going to the apartment only to sleep.

Saturday night the desk clerk told me about the city health officials he let into my unit while I was away. They were checking all of the apartments since many older people were suffering heat strokes. Some bodies lay unclaimed at a large meat refrigeration unit being used as a temporary morgue. Physicians and other health care workers were being recalled from vacation. This was becoming an emergency.

The desk clerk assured me he knew where to ship my body if I were found dead. I promised to stay alive until I left the next day for America. We laughed but it wasn't funny. My five days were almost at an end. I was hot. I was lonely. I longed to go home.

After my final morning visit to the *boulangerie*, I wrote a thank-you note to the apartment owner. It hadn't been so bad. On sudden impulse I scrubbed the pink Crocs and left them by the note. Somehow I felt she would appreciate their novelty. Again I put on the suit and pumps I traveled in and went slowly down to a waiting taxi. No more Metro. I could splurge I was done. I ignored the air-conditioning and rolled down the windows to feel Paris on my face one last time, so glad to be going home.

My family met me in San Francisco with papers filled with news of the European heat wave. In the cool Bay Area evening it seemed already unreal. Mine was a unique experience and it was good to be home.

The very next day I taught my grandson the words to August in Paris and I went shopping for a new pair of Crocs to wear on my upcoming trip to Crete.

*Vocabulary references:

mobile – cell phone

bien sûr – of course

EN VACANCE – on vacation

boulangerie – bakery for breads;

Croque McDo – McDonald's version of the Croque Monsieiur, a ham and cheese melt, not sold in U.S.

April in Paris parody – "August in Paris, baked like a small loaf, I am a French fry, sizzling sweetbreads…."

pissoir – a public urinal usually enclosed by a wall or screen

jolie Americaine – pleasant American

A Croc

I KNOW YOU
Kristina Yates

'I know you,' I said
You're the one who
Left right after you saw me
For the first and last time
Fresh out of the womb
In Mound Park Hospital
St. Petersburg, Florida
May 26, 1950
I was one day old
How scared or numb
Does a father have to be
To leave a newborn girl
And never look back
Did you ever think of me
Or were you able to lock that door behind you
I rarely thought of you
Saying to those who asked
'you don't miss what you didn't know'
I've carried your name Ray Yates all these years
Kristina Rae Yates
You are in me
Though you've never seen me since that day
Sixty years ago

NORMAL
Kristina Yates

It was in the fall of 1968, my senior year. That day I entered the P.E. changing room, looked around, and walked out the back door of the school. Getting into our old Nash Ambassador I drove up the steep hill to the two-bedroom, red-shingled house Mother had built with the FHA loan.

From my dresser drawer I took the tiny package I'd purchased yesterday at the drug store. I got the pint of Jack Daniels whiskey from the bottom cabinet in the kitchen. Mother rarely drank, but said it was important to have alcohol in the house and to know she didn't have to touch it.

Getting back in the car I headed in the direction of West Knoxville, past the residential neighborhoods, shopping malls, until I was in the country where I found a narrow road. I drove down it and pulled the car into the woods.

Turning the engine off, without hesitation I unscrewed the top from the whiskey and drank straight from the bottle, shivering from the intensity of the alcohol. Not a taste I was familiar with.

Putting the whiskey bottle aside, I went into my purse and took out the small package. I slipped the clean new shiny razor blade out of the top of the case which I had purchased yesterday. Holding the blade in my right hand I quickly drew it across the inside of my left wrist. Again and again I made a deep line pulling across my wrist. The blood began to squirt onto the upholstery of the Nash Ambassador. Tendons, which looked like cut flat rubber bands, began to show as they poked from the opening.

Eventually the flow subsided. Blood covered my light tan-colored fake suede skirt and the car upholstery, but the bleeding was slowing down, stopping. Now what do I do. This isn't working. I put the used blade back in the bottom of its container and started the engine. I began to back the car out of the wooded area. Steering with my right hand and resting my bloody left arm and hand on my lap as the skirt continued to drink up the dark red blood. I made my way back to the road and somehow instinctively knew the way back home to South Knoxville. Feeling weak and dizzy I pulled the car over to the side of the road a couple of times so I wouldn't faint. Twenty minutes later I pulled the car into our black asphalt driveway, got out, and entered the house through the side door, which is the one we always used. Carefully holding my left arm against my body, trying not to drip blood onto our clean kitchen floor I made my way into Mother's room and picked up the receiver of the telephone.

Today was the day Mother had scheduled an appointment for me to see Reverend Overton, a Presbyterian minister who was trained in counseling. One day she abruptly said, "Kristina, you're depressed and I want you to see Reverend Overton." That's why I had the car today, so I could drive myself to the appointment after school.

I dialed Reverend Overton's phone number. It was only two o'clock and my appointment wasn't until three. The secretary answered cheerfully, "Rev. Overton's office."

"This is Kristina Yates. I have a three o'clock appointment but wondered if I could come early."

"Reverend Overton is with someone right now, but you are welcome to come and wait," she said.

"Thanks, I'll be there soon."

Leaving a faint trail of red drips, I got in the car and drove to Reverend Overton's office for the first time. I walked into the office, covered in blood, and said to the secretary "I'm Kristina Yates." She got up from behind her desk and pointing to a chair said, "Have a seat, I'll be right back." She left the room and came back with gauze and tape for bandaging. Reverend Overton entered the room and said to me "We're going to have to call your mother, so why don't you think about that and I'll be back shortly." That was my first meeting with Reverend Overton. He went back to the client he was with and the secretary proceeded to bandage up my wrist.

When Reverend Overton was finished with his client we drove to the hospital and mother met us there. It took them four hours of surgery to sew up my wrist. They used a local anesthesia and I remember hearing a nurse say "And she is so young." My arm was in a cast after the surgery.

While I faced the wall in my hospital bed pretending to be asleep, Mother sat in a chair beside my bed. She said to me: "There's nothing worse than trying to kill yourself and then you have to live through it." She said it as if she knew from experience. I remembered her telling me about the time she had taken an overdose of sleeping pills and my grandfather walked her all night, making her drink coffee to keep her from going to sleep. Somehow I felt very close to Mother right then.

A few days after the surgery there was a meeting in a conference room at the hospital: me, Reverend Overton, and several doctors. We sat in a circle with a microphone in the middle and the focus on me. One doctor said 'Tell me about your problems."

"I don't have any problems," I said.

"Well, you're a beautiful young woman and you've just done a very violent thing to yourself."

I didn't respond to his statement.

Reverend Overton said it was important to tell the truth to people who asked what had happened. He said if I wasn't honest that I might try and hide the scar with a bracelet or long sleeves and never feel really comfortable. So Monday morning before school, I called gossipy Martha Walker, my classmate.

"Martha, I'm gonna be late to school today and I was wondering if you could help me out. You see, I was depressed and cut my wrist and I thought if you would spread the word then I wouldn't have to explain to so many people."

"Couldn't we just tell them you cut it slicing tomatoes?"

"Martha, I've got a cast on my arm. That doesn't happen slicing tomatoes."

"Oh, Okay, see you in class."

By third period no one knew what had happened. In fact one boy jokingly said to me, "What happened, did you try to kill yourself?" When asked, I would rotely recite my pat answer: "I was depressed and cut my wrist." A common response from adults was "Well, we all make mistakes."

I thought, "Yeah, mine was not succeeding."

The first time I unwrapped the bandage after the cast was off, black stitches and puckered skin stared back at me. I was told to soak it in warm salt water. I could only move my fingers about a quarter of an inch, and the doctor said they didn't know how much use of my hand I would have.

Janet Welton, a friend in my class, came over and washed my hair for me since I only had one usable arm. She sat and talked with me as I soaked my wrist.

In one of our counseling sessions Reverend Overton asked me to sit on his lap. His intent was to be a father figure, but I was 17 years old, and had never seen my father, or ever had a father figure. I felt even more numb.

"Kristina, we're gonna knit our Christmas presents this year. It will help you regain the use of that hand. Here's a pattern for a little stuffed dog. You knit two sides, sew them together and put cotton batting inside. We can knit house slippers too."

I knitted the presents. Time passed. My hand got better and I was one of four students chosen to be commencement speaker, based on tryouts where we delivered a short speech and several teachers judged us. I graduated with honors and went on to Berea College that summer.

I asked Mother why Reverend Overton had all those doctors sit around and ask me questions in the hospital. "He wanted to make sure they agreed with his diagnosis." "What was the diagnosis," I asked. "Normal teenage depression," she replied.

DINER
Andrea Yee

The bald-headed monster with fire-red eyes lunged at me with steam hissing out of its nostrils, curdling the skin of my neck. I was choking in its saliva. With claws sharp as knives, it clawed at my shoulder and growled...

"Get up, get up, we're late!" It was my father's graveling voice. And it was his large calloused hand shaking my shoulders from the nightmare's grip. The monster retreated back into the dark corner of my ceiling, leaving a trail of sand in my head.

The old Plymouth was honking outside. It was past 5:00 a.m., and we were terribly late for work. In the dark, I stumbled out the door, nearly falling over my two brothers asleep in the living room, and Mama was too exhausted from the week of work to stir.

In the car, Baba was pumping the gas pedal with his foot and frowning at all the dials. The cranking "grrrn-grrrn-grrrrning" engine coughed smoke out of its tailpipe. I closed my eyes and took a deep breath. The cold crisp air cleared the sand in my head, and I grumbled "vroom-vroom-vroom," -- the sound my brothers made racing their toy cars. It worked -- the old car VROOMed back at me! I made a promise I would polish her with a very soft cloth next time.

I jumped out of the smoke curling around my ankles and into the seat beside Baba. His foot was heavy on the gas pedal as I held onto the flaking armrest. The streets glistened in the dampness with the street lamps lit like bowing angels, all standing in a row with oblong halos at their feet, lighting our way. I was remembering when I was twelve how I used to love driving to work with Baba every Saturday morning. I felt as free and important as a grownup with my hand hanging out the window sifting the wind. But that feeling was gone now. The girls' badminton team and band practice was on Saturdays, too, at my new high school.

Baba glanced down with a smile at the algebra book that was opened on my lap. His shoulders shifted back with a deep breath. A word seemed to take shape on his lips. He had never before inquired about how I was doing in school, because that would just invite boasting, which was unacceptable. I was always at the top of my class, but that was simply expected. Perhaps he had a flowery word for me, I thought, words like beautiful, love, wonderful, or terrific. Recently, I had been hearing parents of my new friends sprinkle them on their children daily, like fertilizer. Even during school lunch time, such praises would be heaped on anyone with a new sweater or hairdo or for something as silly as a passing grade. I wanted to join in.

Baba moistened his lips but the words did not come out. I slumped into my seat feeling invisible, wishing my brothers could take my place. To make them grow up faster, at dinner time, I made them finish every single grain of rice in their bowl with extra servings.

We pulled into a brightly lit gas station. Baba stepped out to open his gas cap when the attendant, wearing greasy overalls, approached. Through the windshield, I could see their mouths talking. Baba pointed to the gas pump trying to say "Ethyl," which probably sounded like "etow" in his poor English. The attendant, crossing his arms across his huge chest, scrunched up his face as if he didn't understand. I jumped out of the car to hear him mutter something about "damn stupid chinaman."

I shouted in my thin voice, "My father is just trying to say…"

But Baba interrupted, "*Mo yau guan see, Jie Jie*, (It is not important, big sister)."

Under the bright lights, Baba stood straight with his chest up high. His eyes looked like dark cannons shooting out of his firm jaw. He took one large step toward the surprised attendant, brushing him aside as if he was dandruff, and slid back into the car. The Plymouth poured out smoke. Baba gripped the wheel so hard his knuckles turned white and all the fresh and old wounds from burns and cuts seemed to pop up. I stared out my window because, with each passing street lamp shining on his hand, a pain would flicker in my eye and sit on my chest.

"*Jie Jie, nei hau ma* (are you all right)?" Baba asked softly.

"Just allergy, Baba," was all I could mumble. I bit hard on my quivering lower lip and turned away, fumbling with the hanky Baba handed to me.

Finally, we arrived at the diner late. Baba unloaded the Plymouth, while I turned on electricity with loud click-click-clicks, sending mice and other creatures scampering for cover. The lights, grill, fryer, heater, vent fans, and dishwasher were soon churning their sounds and smells. The coffee urn sat magnificently in the middle of the dining room with its copper dome polished like a bald Buddha on a throne, gurgling and hissing.

I tied on a clean white apron doubled at the waist. The order book flapped in the pocket, a sharpened pencil hooked over my ear, and my ponytail swished side to side: I was ready.

The last click of the switch shot out DINER in blue effervescing neon. It silently screamed up and down the sleepy street. Our regular customers straggled in. Having spent a sleepless night in their unheated rooms of the drafty rooming house across the alley, they were looking for the warmth of the diner. They were cranky because we were late and they were shivering.

But the magic of the very first cup of coffee always had amazing results. As the aroma rose up to through their nostrils, their crosshatched necks grew out of their collars like turtles. Sour lips melted into wide smiles. Because Baba's grill was still not hot enough to make hash browns, I had to buy time with many extra coffee refills, extra toast with jam and butter. Not that these regulars were in a hurry -- they just liked being treated as if they had important matters to tend to after eating breakfast and after reading the newspaper from front to back.

Finally, breakfast was ready: Danny's poached eggs slightly hard so he could dip his toast without dripping it all over his stained jacket; Carl's soft boiled eggs with no bacon because he misplaced his false teeth; Max's milk egg toast with boiled potato for ulcers; Hangover Bob's tomato soup with hard boiled egg and lots of crackers. Since we were closed on Sundays, extra servings of hash browns and toast usually ended up wrapped with napkins and stuffed into their pockets. Sometimes, someone would stroll into the kitchen and joke with Baba, hoping for a bag of leftovers that didn't get cooked into the Soup of the Day. Business, in fact, had been very slow, and the soup became thick and delicious.

These were Baba's loyal customers, poor, but rich with stories. It was Mr. Schwartz's story, though, that I knew the best, because I sat down in the booth with him to cut his meal into bite-sized pieces. He was so crippled he could barely move, or even chew. But every day, without fail, dressed in an outsized suit, he inched painfully to the diner. I learned that he had lived in a camp during the war in Germany, where his whole family had disappeared. He wanted me to remember his story, even though I couldn't imagine something so sad. He could recite poetry, history, Shakespeare, even jokes. Some things are very important, he always told me with a wink and a tip.

I looked at my watch. He was late for breakfast. Maybe, just getting slower.

I was passing by the kitchen when I heard a knife land on the long wooden counter with a "blok," splitting the soup bone no more than one inch away from Baba's fingers. It was the bone breaker, a small version of the guillotine sword. All the other knives were standing in a row behind a slat, looking like convicts standing against the wall: the long blunt turkey slicer, the elegant French knife, the blocky Chinese cleaver, the skinny fish filleter, the toothed bread slicer, a bunch of paring knives, and the slot for the bone breaker. My teeth hurt with each "blok."

Next, the Chinese cleaver, the favorite, was pulled out in one hand and the knife sharpening baton in the other, and, like a conductor, Baba sawed the blade of the knife until it sang like a shrill bird. Then he ran the sharpened blade tip all the way down the wooden counter -- "d-d-d-d-d-d-d-dook." The french knife was next. In this manner the sharpness of all the knives was tested -- "d-d-d-d-d-d-dook."

From my pocket of tips, I put a nickel into our jukebox. It faced the front entrance, sitting like an enticing fat lady, gleaming in blue, red, and yellow jewels. She filled the room with music. I chose a Chubby Checker song, and turned up the volume. Baba joined in with his rhythm section of pots and pans orchestra hanging above him. He reached up with the ladle in one hand and a knife in the other and whacked them until they swayed and rang out: the shallow fry pan – "blam, blammity-blam." Then the soup pot – "bong, bong, bong." The sauce pan – "poong, poong, poong." On and on it went until all the pots, pans, and knives, dancing down the wooden counter, were in tune with the beat: "blam, bong, poong, dong, clang, clangity-dook, clangity-dook, d-d-d-d-d-d-bong, blam, poong, d-d-d-d-d-d-d-bong, blam, poong!"

Before I could slip in another nickel to start another record, Baba launched into his Chinese opera. Luckily, there were no customers -- I hated apologizing for the strange music coming out of the kitchen. But something was different from before -- the words to the opera were not about the usual wars and kings and maidens. The sound was different too. Baba sang louder than ever before. His face turned red. The veins in his neck popped out. His hands gestured wildly to the spirits below. He banged the pots to the spirits above. He lit incense and candles to the red altar housing the God of Fortune and cried out to his dead ancestors.

Baba was desperate. Rent: it was long overdue. We needed a good lunch crowd urgently.

I rushed around setting up for lunch time. Dishes were stacked, and sugar, salt, pepper, and ketchup were refilled. The cash register was checked and newspapers refolded. The soup had to be hot and the butter cold, the salad crisp and the buns soft, and the coffee freshly brewed. The booth reserved for Mr. Schwartz was still set – plate, fork, spoon, napkin, coffee cup.

Just as I was scribbling on the blackboard the Special of the Day, I heard an ambulance approach. Its siren blended into a strange cry with Baba's singing, as it whizzed by and turned the corner. Slowing down, it made another turn into the alley behind us. It stopped. Baba stopped singing. We rushed out the back door of the kitchen and watched the men carry a gurney and black leather bag into the rooming house. Baba followed them inside.

I returned to the diner. Anxious to greet hungry customers strolling by I repolished the front glass panes. But the street was empty. It was nearly noon and Baba hadn't shown up yet.

Suddenly, the diner went dark and silent: the fan vents clicked off, the coffee urn stopped gurgling, the blue neon sign faded. Baba approached the front entrance and started to turn the sign hanging on the front glass pane from OPEN to CLOSED.

"No, Baba, no, no, no," I shouted in a high-pitched, shaking voice. I flipped the sign back to OPEN and stood firm, blocking the entrance door open. My legs were shaking and I stopped breathing. I had never defied Baba before. But his eyes did not meet mine.

Instead, his eyes grew dark like canons again, and he whispered, *"Mo yau guan si le* (this place is not important anymore)" and locked the door.

He put his scarred hand on my shoulder and gently led me to the reserved booth for Mr. Schwartz. The table and both sides of the booth were stacked high with his books and my name scribbled inside.

"Yau quan si (this is important)," Baba's eyes told me. They filled with tears as he cleared away the place setting and unused coffee cup.